AUSTRIAN NOVELISTS

Franz Kafka, Bertha Von Suttner, Stefan Zweig, Robert Musil, Hugo Von Hofmannsthal, Elfriede Jelinek, Thomas Bernhard, Waris Dirie, Gregor Von Rezzori, Walter Von Molo, Ludwig Anzengruber, Joseph Roth, Joseph Delmont, Heimito Von Doderer

BOOKS LLC

Publication Data:

Title: Austrian Novelists

Subtitle: Franz Kafka, Bertha Von Suttner, Stefan Zweig, Robert Musil, Hugo Von Hofmannsthal, Elfriede Jelinek, Thomas Bernhard, Waris Dirie, Gregor Von Rezzori, Walter Von Molo, Ludwig Anzengruber, Joseph Roth, Joseph Delmont, Heimito Von Doderer

Published by: Books LLC, Memphis, Tennessee, USA in 2010

Copyright (chapters): http://creativecommons.org/licenses/by-sa/3.0

Online edition: http://en.wikipedia.org/wiki/Category:Austrian_novelists

Contact the publisher: http://booksllc.net/contactus.cfm

CONTENTS

iii

Introduction

The online edition of this book is at http://booksllc.net/?q=Category:Austrian%5Fnovelists. It's hyperlinked and may be updated. Where we have recommended related pages, you can read them at http://booksllc.net/?q= followed by the page's title. Most entries in the book's index also have a dedicated page at http://booksllc.net/?q= followed by the index entry.

Each chapter in this book ends with a URL to a hyperlinked online version. Use the online version to access related pages, websites, footnote URLs. You can click the history tab on the online version to see a list of the chapter's contributors. While we have included photo captions in the book, due to copyright restrictions you can only view the photos online. You also need to go to the online edition to view some formula symbols or foreign language characters.

The online version of this book is part of Wikipedia, a multilingual, web-based encyclopedia.

Wikipedia is written collaboratively. Since its creation in 2001, Wikipedia has grown rapidly into one of the largest reference web sites, attracting nearly 68 million visitors monthly. There are more than 91,000 active contributors working on more than 15 million articles in more than 270 languages. Every day, hundreds of thousands of active from around the world collectively make tens of thousands of edits and create thousands of new articles.

After a long process of discussion, debate, and argument, articles gradually take on a neutral point of view reached through consensus. Additional editors expand and contribute to articles and strive to achieve balance and comprehensive coverage. Wikipedia's intent is to cover existing knowledge which is verifiable from other sources. The ideal Wikipedia article is well-written, balanced, neutral, and encyclopedic, containing comprehensive, notable, verifiable knowledge.

Wikipedia is open to a large contributor base, drawing a large number of editors from diverse backgrounds. This allows Wikipedia to significantly reduce regional and cultural bias found in many other publications, and makes it very difficult for any group to censor and impose bias. A large, diverse editor base also provides access and breadth on subject matter that is otherwise inaccessible or little documented.

Think you can improve the book? If so, simply go to the online version and suggest changes. If accepted, your additions could appear in the next edition!

1

ALBERT EHRENSTEIN

Albert Ehrenstein (1886, Ottakring, Vienna 1950, New York) was an Austrian-born German Expressionist poet. His poetry exemplifies rejection of bourgeois values and fascination with the Orient, particularly with China. He spent most of his life in Berlin, but also travelled widely across Europe, Africa, and the Far East. In 1930, he travelled to Palestine, and published his impressions in a series of articles. Shortly before the Nazi take-over, Ehrenstein moved to Switzerland, and in 1941 to New York, where he died.

Selected Works

Poetry

- *Der Mensch Schreit* (1916)
- *Die rote Zeit* (1917)
- *Briefe an Gott* (1922)
- *Das gelbe Lied* (1933) adaptation of Chinese poetry

Fiction

- *Tubutsch* (1911)
- *Der Selbstmord eines Katers* (1912)
- *Ritter des Todes* (1926)
- *Gedichte und Prosa* (posthumous edition Jerusalem: 1961)

References (URLs online)

- *Ehrenstein, Albert*, article in Encyclopaedia Judaica.
- Beigel, A. *Erlebnis und Flucht im Werk Albert Ehrensteins* (1966).

See also: Ehrenstein

A hyperlinked version of this chapter is at http://booksllc.net?q=Albert% 5FEhrenstein

ALFRED KUBIN

Alfred Leopold Isidor Kubin (April 10, 1877 August 20, 1959) was an Austrian Expressionist, illustrator and occasional writer.

Biography

Kubin was born in Bohemia in the town of Litomice, which was then part of the Austro-Hungarian Empire. From 1892 to 1896, he was apprenticed to the landscape photographer Alois Beer, although he learned little.[1] In 1896, he attempted suicide on his mother's grave, and a short stint in the Austrian army the following year ended with a nervous breakdown.[1] In 1898, Kubin began a period of artistic study at a private academy run by the painter Ludwig Schmitt-Reutte, before enrolling at the Munich Academy in 1899, without finishing his studies there. In Munich, Kubin discovered the works of Odilon Redon, Edvard Munch, James Ensor, Henry de Groux and Félicien Rops. He was profoundly affected by the prints of Max Klinger, and later recounted: "Here a new art was thrown open to me, which offered free play for the imaginative expression of every conceivable world of feeling. Before putting the engravings away I swore that I would dedicate my life to the creation of similar works".[2] The aquatint technique used by Klinger and Goya influenced the style of his works of this period, which are mainly ink and wash drawings of fantastical, often macabre subjects.[1] Kubin produced a small number of oil paintings in the years between 1902 and 1910, but thereafter his output consisted of pen and ink drawings, watercolors, and lithographs. In 1911, he became associated with the *Blaue Reiter* group, and exhibited with them in the *Galerie Der Sturm* exhibition in Berlin in 1913.[2] After that time, he lost contact with the artistic avant-garde.

He is considered an important representative of Symbolism and Expressionism, noted for dark, spectral, symbolic fantasies (often assembled into thematic series of drawings). Like Oskar Kokoschka and Albert Paris Gütersloh, Kubin had both artistic and literary talent. He illustrated works by Edgar Allan Poe, E.T.A. Hoffmann, Fyodor Dostoevsky and others. He was also the author of several books, the best known being his novel *Die Andere Seite* (*The Other Side*) (1909), an apocalyptic fantasy set in an oppressive imaginary land which has an atmosphere of claustrophobic absurdity reminiscent of the writings of Franz Kafka.

His literary works also include:

- *The Looking Box*, 1925;
- *Of the Desk of a Draughtsman*, 1939;
- *Adventure of an Indication Feather/Spring*, 1941;
- *Sober Balladen*, 1949;
- *Evening-red*, 1950;
- *Fantasies in the Boehmerwald*, 1951;
- *Daemons and Night Faces*, 1959 (autobiography).

From 1906 until his death, he lived a withdrawn life in a small castle on a twelfth century estate in Zwickledt, Upper Austria. In 1938, at the Anschluss of Austria and Nazi Germany, his work was declared entartete Kunst ('degenerate art'), but he managed to go on working during World War II. Kubin was awarded the Great Austrian State Prize in 1951, and the Austrian Decoration for Science and Art in 1957.

Notes

- 1. Oxford Art Online
- 2. Arnason & Wheeler 1986, p. 88.

See also (online edition)

- List of Austrian artists and architects
- List of Austrians

References (URLs online)

- Arnason, H. H., & Wheeler, D. (1986). *History of modern art: Painting, sculpture, architecture, photography.* Englewood Cliffs, N.J.: Prentice -Hall. ISBN 233676248
- Assman, Peter *Alfred Kubin 1877-1959* Exhibition catalogue Brussels (Ixelles) 1997
- *Alfred Kubin* Exhibition catalogue Neue Galerie New York 2008
- Romana Schuler *Alfred Kubin, Aus meinem Reich* Exhibition catalogue Leopold Museum Vienna 2003
- *Traumgestalten. 100 Meisterwerke aus dem Besitz der Graphischen Sammlung Albertina* Vienna 1990

Websites (URLs online)

- www.alfred-kubin.com (in German)
- *Water Spirit*: oil painting by Alfred Kubin

A hyperlinked version of this chapter is at http://booksllc.net?q=Alfred%5FKubin

3

ALOISIA KIRSCHNER

Aloisia Kirschner (June 17, 1854 - February 10, 1934) was an Austrian novelist, born in Prague and favorably known under her pseudonym **Ossip Schubin**, which she borrowed from the novel *Helena* by Ivan Turgenev.

Brought up on her parent's estate at Lochkov, she afterward spent several winters in Brussels, Paris, and Rome, receiving there, undoubtedly, many inspirations for her clever descriptions of artistic Bohemianism and international fashionable society, which were her favorite themes. An uncommonly keen observer, her great gift for striking characterization, frequently seasoned with sarcasm, is especially apparent in her delineations of the military and artistic circles in Austria-Hungary.

She died in 1934 at Schloss Kosatek, Bohemia.

Works

Her works are of unequal quality, the earlier being the best. The more important of her novels and stories include:

- *Ehre* (1882; seventh edition, 1893)
- *Die Geschichte eines Genies: Die Galbrizzi* (1884)
- *Unter uns* (1884; fourth edition, 1892)
- *Gloria Victis* (1885; third edition, 1892)
- *Erlachof* (1887)
- *Es fiel ein Reif in der Frühlingsnacht* (fourth edition, 1901)
- *Asbeïn, aus dem Leben eines Virtuosen* (1888; fourth edition, 1901), and its sequel, *Boris Lensky* (1889; third edition, 1897), probably her most meritorious work
- *Unheimliche Geschichten* (1889)
- *O du mein Oesterreich!* (1890; third edition, 1897)
- *Finis Poloni* (1893)
- *Toter Frühling* (1893)
- *Gebrochene Flügel* (1894)
- *Die Heimkehr* (1897)
- *Slawische Liebe* (1900)
- *Marska* (1902)
- *Refugium peccatorum* (1903)
- *Der Gnadenschuss* (1905)
- *Der arme Nicki* (1906)
- *Primavera* (1908)
- *Miserere nobis* (1910)

Websites (URLs online)

- Works by Ossip Schubin at Internet Archive. Scanned, illustrated original editions.

This article incorporates text from an edition of the New International Encyclopedia *that is in the public domain.*

A hyperlinked version of this chapter is at http://booksllc.net?q=Aloisia%5FKirschner

4

ANNEMARIE SELINKO

Annemarie Selinko (September 1, 1914 - July 28, 1986) was an Austrian novelist who wrote a number of best-selling books in German from the 1930s through the 1950s. Although she had been based in Germany, in 1939 at the start of World War II she took refuge in Denmark with her Danish husband, but then in 1943, they again became refugees, this time to Sweden. [1] [2]

Many of her novels have been adapted into movies and all have been translated into numerous languages. Her last work *Désirée* (1951) was about Désirée Clary, one of Napoleon's lovers and, later, a queen of Sweden. It has been translated into 25 languages and in 1956 was turned into a movie with Marlon Brando and Jean Simmons. It is dedicated to her sister Liselotte, who was murdered by the Nazis.

Bibliography

Novels

- *Ich war ein häßliches Mädchen* (*I Was an Ugly Girl*), Vienna: Kirschner Verlag, 1937; Made into a film, West Germany, 1955.
- *Morgen wird alles besser* (*Tomorrow is Always Better*), 1941; Made into a film, Morgen gaat het beter, Netherlands, 1939
- *Heute heiratet mein Mann* (*My Husband Marries Today*), 1943; Made into a film, West Germany, 1956.
- *Désirée*, 1952; Made into a film, U.S., 1954.

A hyperlinked version of this chapter is at http://booksllc.net?q=Annemarie%5FSelinko

5

BERTHA VON SUTTNER

Bertha Felicitas Sophie Freifrau von Suttner (Baroness **Bertha von Suttner**, Gräfin (Countess) Kinsky von Wchinitz und Tettau; 9 June 1843 - 21 June 1914) was an Austrian novelist, radical (organizational) pacifist, and the first woman to be a Nobel Peace Prize laureate.

Biography

Suttner was born in Prague, Bohemia, the daughter of an impoverished Austrian Field Marshal, Franz-Josef Graf Kinsky von Wchinitz und Tettau, and wife Sophie von Körner, and governess to the wealthy Suttner family from 1873. She had an older brother, Arthur Franz Graf Kinsky von Wchinitz und Tettau. She became engaged to engineer and novelist Arthur Gundaccar Freiherr von Suttner (who died on December 10, 1902), but his family opposed the match, and she answered an advertisement from Alfred Nobel in 1876 to become his secretary-housekeeper at his Paris residence. She only remained a week before returning to Vienna and secretly marrying Arthur on June 12, 1876.

Online image: Bertha von Suttner Monument in Wagga Wagga, Australia.

Suttner became a leading figure in the peace movement with the publication of her novel, *Die Waffen nieder!* ("Lay Down Your Arms!") in 1889 and founded an Austrian pacifist organization in 1891. She gained international repute as editor of the international pacifist journal *Die Waffen nieder!*, named after her book, from 1892 to 1899. Her pacifism was influenced by the writings of Henry Thomas Buckle, Herbert Spencer, and Charles Darwin. Though her personal contact with Alfred Nobel had been brief, she corresponded with him until his death in 1896, and it is believed that she was a major influence in his decision to include a peace prize among those prizes provided in his will, which she won in 1905.

A film entitled *Die Waffen nieder* by Holger Madsen and Carl Theodor Dreyer was released by Nordisk Films Kompagni in 1914.

Commemoration on coins and stamps

- Bertha von Suttner was recently selected as a main motif for a high value collectors' coin: the 2008 Europe Taler. The reverse shows important people in the history of Europe, including Bertha von Suttner. Also depicted in the coin are Martin Luther (symbolising the transition from the Middle Ages to the modern period); Antonio Vivaldi (exemplifying the importance of European cultural life); and James Watt (representing the industrialization of Europe, inventor of the first steam engine in the 18th century).

- She is depicted on the Austrian 2 euro coin, and was pictured on the old Austrian 1000 schilling bank note.

- She was commemorated on a 2005 German postage stamp.

Works

- von Suttner, Bertha (1910) (in English). *Memoirs of Bertha von Suttner: The Records of an Eventful Life (Authorized Translation).* Boston and London: Ginn & Co., Published for the International School of Peace.

Notes

Regarding personal names: *Freifrau* (*Baroness*) is a title rather than a first or middle name. It denotes the wife of a *Freiherr*.

See also (online edition)

- List of pacifists
- List of Austrians
- List of Austrian writers

o List of female Nobel laureates

Websites (URLs online)

o Nobel Entry
o More Info from Nobel Winners
o Another biography on Bertha von Suttner
o 2005 the Bertha von Suttner Year
o Works by Bertha von Suttner at Project Gutenberg
o Bertha von Suttner (1910). *Memoirs of Bertha Von Suttner*. Ginn & co..
o "Baroness Bertha von Suttner; Author of "Lay Down Your Arms" and Winner of the Nobel Peace Prize". *New York Times Review of Books*: pp. BR61. February 5, 1911. (PDF of full review of *Memoirs*)
o Claus Bernet: *Bertha von Suttner*. In: *Biographisch-Bibliographisches Kirchenlexikon* (BBKL). Bd. 24, Nordhausen 2005, ISBN 3-88309-247-9, Sp. 14351471. (German)

A hyperlinked version of this chapter is at http://booksllc.net?q=Bertha%5Fvon%5FSuttner

6

EDMUND BLUM

Edmund Blum (* 9. September 1874 in Steinamanger/Szombathely Hungary; 14. April 1938 in Vienna) was an Austrian author and dentist.

Life

Edmund Blum was 1874 born as son of Alexander Blum and Julia Blum born Lazarus. He studied in Vienna, where he 29. April 1898 received a doctorate degree in medicine. He was also writer and publisher.

Career

Blum wrote over 25 books and used also pseudonym E. B. Junkh. 1920 he founded own publishing house called E.B. Seps in Vienna. His first book was *Warum lassen sich die Juden nicht taufen?!"* published by 0. Th. Scholl. Later 1928 he founded a second publishing house Bergis Verlag Wien," where were also another Authors like Max Epstein, Hermann W. Anders, Hellmut Schlien, Fritz

v. Unruh or Berthold Sprung) published. Edmund Blum died 14. April 1938 in Vienna.

Trivia

On 16 June celebrate fans of Irish writer James Joyce across the globe the Blooms-day and since 1994 also in the Hungarian town Szombathely. The names derives from Leopold Bloom, the protagonist of Ulysses. Szombathely is the fictional birthplace of Leopold Bloom's father Rudolf Virag (Virag means in german Blume). In front of the house at 40 Fö Square is a Joyce statue. In this house lived in the second half of 19 century Martin Blum, grandfather of Edmund Blum.

Bibliography

- Warum lassen sich die Juden nicht taufen?! (1913)
- Das Brauthemd (1919)
- Die Gefallene (1920)
- Die Halbjuden (1920)
- Junggesellennot, sexual-psychologischer Roman (1920)
- Die Lüsterne (1922)
- Die Gelegenheitsmacherin (1922)
- Magdas Fehltritt (1923)
- Die Hochzeitsnacht (1923)
- Die Verführte (1923)
- Judenhaß (1923)
- Ohne Wollust (1923)
- Sommerbräutigam
- Die Sumpfblume und andere Wiener Novellen (1923)
- Lebt Gott noch? Krise der Weltanschauung (1928)
- Die Damen Bolzani (1932)
- Des Selbstmörders Schwester (1932)
- Das Eheexperiment (1920)
- Sein Venusdienst (1923)
- Mädis Irrwege (1925)
- Die Verführte (1923)
- Der Hund und die Liebe (1923)
- Treu bis Neapel (1923)
- Die Schande (1923)
- Schach der Liebe (1923)

Websites (URLs online)

- verlagsgeschichte.murrahall
- bloomsday hungary

A hyperlinked version of this chapter is at http://booksllc.net?q=Edmund%5FBlum

7

ELFRIEDE JELINEK

Elfriede Jelinek (German pronunciation: [lfid jlink]) (born 20 October 1946) is an Austrian playwright and novelist. She was awarded the Nobel Prize in Literature in 2004 for her "musical flow of voices and counter-voices in novels and plays that, with extraordinary linguistic zeal, reveal the absurdity of society's clichés and their subjugating power."

Biography

Jelinek was born in Mürzzuschlag, Styria. Her father, a chemist of Jewish-Czech origin ("Jelinek" means "little deer" in Czech) managed to avoid persecution during the Second World War by working in strategically important industrial production. However, several dozen family members became victims of the Holocaust. Her mother, with whom she shared the household even as an adult, and with whom she had a difficult relationship, was from a formerly prosperous Vienna family. As a child, Elfriede suffered from what she considered an over-restrictive education in a Roman Catholic convent school in Vienna. Her mother planned a career as a musical Wunderkind for Elfriede. From an early age, she was instructed in piano, organ, guitar, violin, viola and recorder. Later, she went on to study at the Vienna Conservatory, where she graduated with an organist diploma. Jelinek also studied art history and drama at the University of Vienna. However, she had to discontinue her studies due to an anxiety disorder that prevented her from following courses.

Jelinek started writing poetry at a young age. She made her literary debut with the collection *Lisas Schatten* in 1967.

In the early 1970s, Jelinek married Gottfried Hüngsberg.

Work and politics

Prior to winning the Nobel Prize, her work was largely unknown outside the German-speaking world and was said to resemble that of acclaimed Austrian playwright Thomas Bernhard, with its pathology of destruction and its concomitant comedic abrogation. In fact, despite the author's own differentiation from Austria, Jelinek's writing is deeply rooted in the tradition of Austrian literature, showing the influence of Austrian writers such as Ingeborg Bachmann and Robert Musil.

Jelinek's political positions (in particular her feminist stance and her party affilia- tions) are of vital importance to any assessment of her work. They are also a part of the reason for the vitriolic controversy surrounding Jelinek and her work.

Brief history of Jelinek's political engagements

Jelinek was a member of Austria's Communist Party from 1974 to 1991. Jelinek became a household name during the 1990s due to her vociferous clash with Jörg Haider's far-right Freedom Party. Following the 1999 National Council elections and the subsequent formation of a coalition cabinet consisting of the Freedom Party and the Austrian People's Party, Jelinek became one of the new cabinet's most vocal critics. Citing the Freedom Party's alleged nationalism and authoritarianism, many European and overseas administrations swiftly decided openly to ostracize Austria's administration. The cabinet construed the sanctions against it as directed against Austria as such and attempted to prod the nation into a national rallying (*Nationaler Schulterschluss*) behind the coalition parties. This provoked a temporary heating of the political climate severe enough for dissidents such as Jelinek to be accused of treason by coalition supporters. She also petitioned for the release of Jack Unterweger, who was imprisoned for the murder of a prostitute, as a model of social reform. Immediately following his successful release he went on to murder ten more women in two years and committed suicide after arrest.

Jelinek's work

Jelinek's work is multi-faceted and highly controversial. It has been by turns praised and condemned by leading literary critics (in the wake of the Fritzl case, for example, she was accused of "executing 'hysterical' portraits of Austrian perversity"[1]). Likewise, her political activism evokes divergent and often heated reactions. Despite the public controversy surrounding her work, Jelinek has won many distinguished prizes, among them are the Georg Büchner Prize in 1998; the Mülheim Dramatists Prize in 2002 and 2004; the Franz Kafka Prize in 2004; and the Nobel Prize in Literature, also in 2004.

Prevalent topics in her prose and dramatic works are female sexuality, its abuse and the battle of the sexes in general. Texts such as *Wir sind Lockvögel, Baby!* (*We are Decoys, Baby!*), *Die Liebhaberinnen* (*Women as Lovers*) and *Die Klavierspielerin* (*The Pianist*) showcase the brutality and power play inherent in human relations in a style that is at times ironically formal and tightly controlled. According to Jelinek, power and aggression are often the principal driving forces of relationships. Her provocative novel *Lust* contains graphically-delineated descriptions of sexuality, aggression and abuse. It received poor reviews by many critics, some of whom considered it little more than pornography, but was considered misunderstood and undervalued by others, who noted the power of the cold descriptions of moral failures.

In her later work, Jelinek has somewhat abandoned female issues to focus her energy on social criticism in general and Austria's difficulties to owning up to its Nazi past in particular; an example is *Die Kinder der Toten* (*The Children of the Dead*).

Her plays often involve an emphasis on choreography. In *Sportstück*, for example, the issue of violence and fascism in sports is explored. Some consider her plays taciturn, others lavish, and others still a new form of theater altogether.

Jelinek's novel *Die Klavierspielerin* (*The Piano Player*) was filmed with title *The Piano Teacher* by Austrian director Michael Haneke, with French actress Isabelle Huppert as the protagonist.

In late April 2006, Jelinek stood up to protect Peter Handke, whose play *Die Kunst des Fragens* (*The Art of Asking*) was removed from the repertoire of the Comédie-Française for his alleged support of Slobodan Miloevi.

The Nobel Prize

Commenting on the Nobel Prize, she said she felt very happy to receive the Prize, but also felt despair: "despair for becoming a known, a person of the public". Paradigmatic for her modesty and subtle self-irony, she a reputed feminist writer wondered if she had not been awarded the prize mainly for "being a woman" and suggested that among authors writing in German, Peter Handke whom she praises as a "living classic", would have been a more worthy recipient.

Jelinek was criticized for not accepting the prize in person; instead, a video message was presented at the ceremony. Others appreciated that Jelinek openly disclosed that she suffers from agoraphobia and social phobia, anxiety disorders which can be highly disruptive to everyday functioning yet are often concealed by those affected out of shame or feeling of inadequacy. Jelinek has said that her anxiety disorders make it impossible for her even to go to the cinema or to board an airplane (in an interview she wished to be able to fly to New York to see the skyscrapers one day before dying), and she felt incapable of taking part in any ceremony. However, in her own words as stated in another tape message: "I would also very much like to be in Stockholm, but I cannot move as fast and far as my language."

In 2005, Knut Ahnlund left the Swedish Academy in protest, describing Jelinek's work as "whining, unenjoyable public pornography" as well as "a mass of text shoveled together without artistic structure". He said later her selection for the prize "has not only done irreparable damage to all progressive forces, it has also confused the general view of literature as an art".[2]

Bibliography

Novels

- *bukolit. hörroman*; Wien 1979 ISBN 3853940234
- *wir sind lockvögel baby!*; Reinbek 1970 ISBN 349912341X
- *Michael. Ein Jugendbuch für die Infantilgesellschaft*; Reinbek 1972 ISBN 3499250128
- *Die Liebhaberinnen*; Reinbek 1975 ISBN 3499250640
- *Die Ausgesperrten*; Reinbek 1980 ISBN 349803314X
- *Die Klavierspielerin*; Reinbek 1983 ISBN 3498033166
- *Oh Wildnis, oh Schutz vor ihr*; Reinbek 1985 ISBN 3499134071
- *Lust*; Reinbek 1989 ISBN 3498033239
- *Die Kinder der Toten*; Reinbek 1997 ISBN 3499221616
- *Greed*; Reinbek 2000 ISBN 349923131X
- *Neid: Privatroman*; 2007

Plays

- *Was geschah, nachdem Nora ihren Mann verlassen hatte; oder Stützen der Gesellschaften (What Happened after Nora Left Her Husband; or Pillars of Society)* premiered in Graz, Austria (October 1979) With Kurt Josef Schildknecht as director.
- *Clara S, musikalische Tragödie (Clara S, a Musical Tragedy)* Premiered at Bonn (1982) OCLC 41445178

o *Burgtheater. Posse mit Gesang (Burgtheater. Farce with Songs)* Premiered at Bonn (1985)
o *Begierde und Fahrererlaubnis (eine Pornographie) (Desire and Permission To Drive - Pornography)* Premiered at the Styrian Autumn, Graz (1986)
o *Krankheit oder Moderne Frauen. Wie ein Stück (Illness or Modern Women. Like a Play)* Premiered at Bonn, (1987) ISBN 9783922009887
o *Präsident Abendwind. Ein Dramolett, sehr frei nach Johann Nestroy (President Abendwind. A dramolet, very freely after Johann Nestroy)* Premiered at the Tyrol Landestheater, Innsbruck (1992)
o *Wolken. Heim (Clouds. Home)* Premiered at Bonn (1988) ISBN 9783882431476
o *Totenauberg.* Premiered at the Vienna Burgtheater (Akademietheater) (1992) ISBN 9783498033262
o *Rastätte oder Sie machens alle. Eine Komödie (Service Area or They're All Doing It. A Comedy)* Premiered at the Burgtheater, Vienna (1994)
o *Stecken, Stab und Stangl. Eine Handarbeit (Rod, Staff, and Crook - Handmade)* Premiered at the Deutsches Schauspielhaus, Hamburg (1996)
o *Ein Sportstück (A Sport Play)* Premiered at the Burgtheater, Vienna (1998)
o *er nicht als er (zu, mit Robert Walser) (him not himself - about/with Robert Walser)* Premiered at the Salzburg Festival in conjunction with the Deutsches Schauspielhaus, Hamburg (1998)
o *Das Lebewohl (Les Adieux)* Premiered at the Berliner Ensemble (2000)
o *Das Schweigen" ("Silence")* Premiered at the Deutsches Schauspielhaus, Hamburg (2000)
o *Der Tod und das Mädchen II (Death and the Maiden II)* Premiered at EXPOL 2000 in Hanover in conjunction with the Saarbrücken Staatstheater and ZKM Karlsruhe (2000) ISBN 9783442761623
o *MACHT NICHTS - Eine Kleine Trilogie des Todes ("NO PROBLEM - A Little Trilogy of Death")* Premiered at the Zürich Schauspielhaus (2001) ISBN 9783499226830
o *In den Alpen ("In the Alps")* Premiered at the Munich Kammerspiele in conjunction with the Zürich Schauspielhaus (2002) Berlin: Berlin Verlag. (2002) 259 pages. ISBN 9783827004574
o *Prinzessinnendramen: Der Tod und das Mädchen I-III und IV-V (Dramas of Princesses: Death and the Maiden I-III and IV-V)* Parts I-III premiered at the Deutsches Schauspielhaus, Hamburg (2002) Parts IV-V premiered at the Deutsches Theater, Berlin (2002)
o *Das Werk. (The Works)* Premiered at the Vienna Burgtheater (Akademietheater) (2003)
o *Bambiland* Premiered at the Burgtheater, Vienna (2003) ISBN 9783498032258
o *Irm und Margit A part of "Attabambi Pornoland"* Premiered at the Zürich Schauspielhaus (2004)
o *Ulrike Maria Stuart* Premiered at Thalia Theater Hamburg (2006)
o *Über Tiere* 2006
o *Rechnitz* (Der Würgeengel) 2008
o *Die Kontrakte des Kaufmanns. Eine Wirtschaftskomödie* (2009)

Translations

o *Die Enden der Parabel* (*Gravity's Rainbow*) novel by Thomas Pynchon; 1976
o *Herrenjagd* Drama by Georges Feydeau; 1983

- *Floh im Ohr* Drama by Georges Feydeau; 1986
- *Der Gockel* Drama by Georges Feydeau; 1986
- *Die Affaire Rue de Lourcine* Drama by Eugène Labiche; 1988
- *Die Dame vom Maxim* Drama by Georges Feydeau; 1990
- *Der Jude von Malta* Drama by Christopher Marlowe; 2001
- *Ernst sein ist alles* Drama by Oscar Wilde; 2004
- Lyrik und Kurzgeschichten (latein)amerikanischer AutorInnen

Opera libretto

- *Lost Highway* (2003), adapted from the film by David Lynch, with music by Olga Neuwirth

Jelinek's novels in English

- *The Piano Teacher* (1988), translation of *Die Klavierspielerin* by Joachim Neugroschel. New York: Weidenfeld & Nicolson, ISBN 9781555840525.
- *Wonderful, Wonderful Times* (1990), translation of *Die Ausgesperrten* by Michael Hulse. London: Serpent's Tail, ISBN 9781852421687.
- *Lust* (1992), translated by Michael Hulse. London: Serpent's Tail, ISBN 9781852421830.
- *Women as Lovers* (1994), translation of *Die Liebhaberinnen* by Martin Chalmers. London: Serpent's Tail, 1994, ISBN 1852422378.
- *Greed* (2006), translation by Martin Chalmers. Serpent's Tail, ISBN 185242902X.

See also (online edition)

- List of female Nobel laureates

References (URLs online)

- 1. "Wife of incest dad under suspicion". The Australian, May 5, 2008.
- 2. "Member's abrupt resignation rocks Nobel Prize community". *Boston Globe*, October 12, 2005.

Websites (URLs online)

- Official website (German)
- Elfriede Jelinek in the German National Library catalogue (German)
- Elfriede Jelinek Nobel Prize Lecture
- Elfriede Jelinek: New German dramatic art. Goethe-Instituts
- Elfriede Jelinek-Forschungszentrum
- Nobel site biography
- BBC synopsis
- Biography at FemBio
- The Weekly Standard: "Oops... They Did It Again" On Elfriede Jelinek being awarded the Nobel Prize for Literature
- Die Gewaltproblematik bei Elfriede Jelinek

○ Elfriede Jelinek: Nichts ist verwirklicht. Alles muss jetzt neu definiert werden. (German)
○ Marjorie Perloff's article Vienna Roast: On Elfriede Jelinek
○ Goethe Institut's entry on Elfriede Jelinek

A hyperlinked version of this chapter is at http://booksllc.net?q=Elfriede%5FJelinek

8

FELIX BRAUN

Felix Braun (November 4, 1885, Vienna November 29, 1973, Klosterneuburg, Lower Austria) was an Austrian writer.

Life

Braun was born in Vienna to a Jewish family. His mother died in 1888 during the birth of his sister, Käthe, who would also become a famous writer. In 1904, he enrolled in German studies, as well as art history, at the University of Vienna, and took his doctorate four years later. His literary publications began to appear in 1905 in the *Neue Freie Presse*, the *Österreichische Rundschau*, and the *Neue Rundschau*. He was appointed arts editor of the Berliner *National-Zeitung* in 1910.

In 1912, Braun married Hedwig Freund, but the couple would divorce in 1915. While working as an editor at Verlag Georg Müller in Munich, he made the acquaintance of a number of important writers, among whom were Hans Carossa, Thomas Mann, and Rainer Maria Rilke. From 1928 to 1938, he was a Privatdozent in German literature at Palermo and Padua. He converted from Judaism to

Catholicism in 1935. To escape persecution by the Nazis, who banned his work, he immigrated in 1939 to the United Kingdom and remained there until 1951, teaching literature and art history. After returning to Austria, Braun lectured at the Max Reinhardt Seminar and the University of Applied Arts Vienna. Braun died in 1973 and was honored with a burial in the Zentralfriedhof of Vienna. In 1977, a lane in Vienna was named after him.

Writing

At the beginning of the 20th century, Braun belonged to the movement known as Young Vienna, where he found the company of such innovative writers as Stefan Zweig, Anton Wildgans, and Max Brod. Braun was a Neo-Romantic, who wrote refined, cultivated poetry in multiple forms. His work centered around the themes of religion, classical antiquity, and his Austrian homeland. Braun also served as secretary to the great Austrian writer Hugo von Hofmannsthal and formed a close friendship with his employer.

Braun edited and published a highly respected anthology of German lyric poetry, called *Der Tausendjährige Rosenstrauch* (*The Thousand-Year Rose Bush*), in 1937. It has been reissued in numerous editions and remains one of the most popular collections of its kind. He also translated the work of Thomas à Kempis and John of the Cross.

Awards and honors

- 1947 Literaturpreis der Stadt Wien
- 1951 Großer Österreichischer Staatspreis für Literatur
- 1955 Ehrenring der Stadt Wien
- 1955 Stiftermedaille des Bundesministeriums für Unterricht
- 1965 Grillparzer-Preis
- 1966 Großes Ehrenzeichen für Kunst und Wissenschaft

Publications

- *Gedichte*, poems, 1909
- *Novellen und Legenden*, 1910
- *Der Schatten des Todes*, novel, 1910
- *Till Eulenspiegels Kaisertum*, comedy, 1911
- *Neues Leben*, poems, 1912
- *Verklärungen*, 1916
- *Tantalos*, tragedy, 1917
- *Die Träume des Vineta*, legends, 1919
- *Hyazinth und Ismene*, dramatic lyrics, 1919
- *Das Haar der Berenike*, poems, 1919
- *Attila*, legend, 1920
- *Aktaion*, tragedy, 1921

- *Die Taten des Herakles*, novel, 1921
- *Wunderstunden*, short stories 1923
- *Der unsichtbare Gast*, novel, 1924, rev. 1928
- *Der Schneeregenbogen*, 1925
- *Das innere Leben*, poems, 1926
- *Deutsche Geister*, essay, 1925
- *Die vergessene Mutter*, short stories, 1925
- *Esther*, play, 1926
- *Der Sohn des Himmels*, mystery play, 1926
- *Agnes Altkirchner*, novel, 1927, rev. 1965
- *Zwei Erzählungen von Kindern*, 1928
- *Die Heilung der Kinder*, short stories, 1929
- *Laterna magica*, short stories and legends, 1932
- *Ein indisches Märchenspiel*, 1935
- *Ausgewählte Gedichte*, 1936
- *Kaiser Karl V.*, tragedy, 1936
- *Der Stachel in der Seele*, novel, 1948
- *Das Licht der Welt*, autobiography, 1949, rev. 1962
- *Die Tochter des Jairus*, drama, 1950
- *Briefe in das Jenseits*, short stories, 1952
- *Aischylos*, dialogue, 1953
- *Viola d'Amore*, selected poems from 1903-1953, 1953
- *Das musische Land*, essays, 1952, rev. 1970
- *Die Eisblume*, essays, 1955
- *Rudolf der Stifter*, drama, 1955
- *Joseph und Maria*, drama, 1956
- *Irina und der Zar*, drama, 1956
- *Orpheus*, tragedy, 1956
- *Unerbittbar bleibt Vergangenheit*, selected works, 1957
- *Gespräch über Stifters Mappe meines Urgroßvaters*, 1958
- *Der Liebeshimmel*, 1959
- *Palermo und Monreale*, 1960
- *Imaginäre Gespräche*, 1960
- *Rede auf Max Mell*, 1960
- *Zeitgefährten, Begegnungen*, 1963
- *Die vier Winde*, Christmas stories, 1964
- *Schönes in Süditalien - Palermo*, essays, 1965
- *Anrufe des Geistes*, essays, 1965
- *Aufruf zur Tafel*, mystery, 1965
- *Das weltliche Kloster*, short stories, 1965
- *Das Nelkenbeet*, poems from 1914-1965, 1965
- *Frühe und späte Dramen 1909-1967*, 1971

References (URLs online)

- Biography from the Österreichisches Literaturarchiv (in German)

Further reading

○ Dencker, Klaus Peter. *Literarischer Jugendstil im Drama: Studien zu Felix Braun.* Vienna: Schendl, 1971. ISBN 3-85268-028-X.

A hyperlinked version of this chapter is at http://booksllc.net?q=Felix%5FBraun

9

FRANZ KAFKA

Franz Kafka (German pronunciation: [fants kafka]; 3 July 1883 3 June 1924) is one of the most influential fiction writers of the early 20th century; a novelist and writer of short stories whose works, only after his death, came to be regarded as one of the major achievements of 20th century literature.

He was born to middle class German-speaking Jewish parents in Prague, Bohemia, now part of the Czech Republic, in what was then the Austro-Hungarian Empire. The house in which he was born, on the Old Town Square next to Prague's Church of St Nicholas, today contains a permanent exhibition devoted to the author.[1]

Kafka's workthe novels *The Trial* (1925), *The Castle* (1926) and *Amerika* (1927), as well as short stories including *The Metamorphosis* (1915) and *In the Penal Colony* (1914)is now collectively considered to be among the most original bodies of work in modern Western literature. Much of his work, unfinished at the time of his death, was published posthumously.[2]

The writer's name has led to the term "Kafkaesque" being used in the English language.

Biography

Online image: Kafka at the age of five

Kafka was born into a middle-class Jewish family in Prague, the capital of Bohemia.

Online image: The former house of Franz Kafka. It now stands as a memorial open to the public without fee, but also contains items related to Kafka and Prague for sale.

His father, Hermann Kafka (18521931), was described as a "huge, selfish, over-bearing businessman"[3] and by Kafka himself as "a true Kafka in strength, health, appetite, loudness of voice, eloquence, self-satisfaction, worldly dominance, endurance, presence of mind, [and] knowledge of human nature". Hermann was the fourth child of Jacob Kafka, a ritual slaughterer, and came to Prague from Osek, a Czech-speaking Jewish village near Písek in southern Bohemia. After working as a traveling sales representative, he established himself as an independent retailer of men's and women's fancy goods and accessories, employing up to 15 people and using a jackdaw (*kavka* in Czech) as his business logo. Kafka's mother, Julie (18561934), was the daughter of Jakob Löwy, a prosperous brewer in Podbrady, and was better educated than her husband.[4]

Franz was the eldest of six children.[5] He had two younger brothers: Georg and Heinrich, who died at the ages of fifteen months and six months, respectively, before Franz was seven; and three younger sisters, Gabriele ("Elli") (18891941), Valerie ("Valli") (18901942), and Ottilie ("Ottla") (18921943). On business days, both parents were absent from the home. His mother helped to manage her husband's business and worked in it as much as 12 hours a day. The children were largely reared by a series of governesses and servants. Franz's relationship with his father was severely troubled as explained in the *Letter to His Father* in which he complained of being profoundly affected by his father's authoritative and demanding character.

During World War II, Franz's sisters were sent with their families to the ód Ghetto and died there or in concentration camps. Ottla was sent to the concentration camp at Theresienstadt and then on 7 October 1943 to the death camp at Auschwitz, where 1267 children and 51 guardians, including Ottla, were gassed to death on their arrival.[6]

Education

Online image: Kinsky Palace where Kafka attended gymnasium and his father later owned a shop

Kafka's first language was German, but he was also fluent in Czech.[7] Later, Kafka acquired some knowledge of French language and culture; one of his favorite authors was Flaubert. From 1889 to 1893, he attended the *Deutsche Knabenschule*, the boys' elementary school at the *Masný trh/Fleischmarkt* (meat market), the street now known as Masná street. His Jewish education was limited to his *Bar Mitzvah* celebration at 13 and going to the synagogue four times a year with his father, which he loathed.[8] After elementary school, he was admitted to the rigorous classics-oriented state *gymnasium, Altstädter Deutsches Gymnasium*, an academic secondary school with eight grade levels, where German was also the language of instruction, at Old Town Square, within the Kinsky Palace. He completed his Maturita exams in 1901.[9]

Admitted to the Charles-Ferdinand University of Prague, Kafka first studied chemistry, but switched after two weeks to law. This offered a range of career possibilities, which pleased his father, and required a longer course of study that gave Kafka time to take classes in German studies and art history. At the university, he joined a student club, named *Lese- und Redehalle der Deutschen Studenten*, which organized literary events, readings and other activities. In the end of his first year of studies, he met Max Brod, who would become a close friend of his throughout his life, together with the journalist Felix Weltsch, who also studied law. Kafka obtained the degree of Doctor of Law on 18 June, 1906 and performed an obligatory year of unpaid service as law clerk for the civil and criminal courts.[2]

Employment

On 1 November 1907, he was hired at the Assicurazioni Generali, a large Italian insurance company, where he worked for nearly a year. His correspondence, during that period, witnesses that he was unhappy with his working time schedulefrom 8 p.m. (20:00) until 6 a.m. (06:00)as it made it extremely difficult for him to concentrate on his writing. On 15 July 1908, he resigned, and two weeks later found more congenial employment with the Worker's Accident Insurance Institute for the Kingdom of Bohemia. The job involved investigating personal injury to industrial workers, and assessing compensation. Management professor Peter Drucker credits Kafka with developing the first civilian hard hat while he was employed at the Worker's Accident Insurance Institute, but this is not supported by any document from his employer.[10] His father often referred to his son's job as insurance officer as a "Brotberuf", literally "bread job", a job done only to pay the bills. While Kafka often claimed that he despised the job, he was a diligent and capable employee. He was also given the task of compiling and composing the annual report and was reportedly quite proud of the results, sending copies to friends and family. In parallel, Kafka was also committed to his literary work. Together with his close friends Max Brod and Felix Weltsch, these three were called "Der enge Prager Kreis", the close Prague circle, which was part of a broader Prague Circle, "a loosely knit group of German-Jewish writers who contributed to the culturally fertile soil of Prague from the 1880s till after World War I."[11]

In 1911, Karl Hermann, spouse of his sister Elli, asked Kafka to collaborate in the operation of an asbestos factory known as Prager Asbestwerke Hermann and Co. Kafka showed a positive attitude at first, dedicating much of his free time to the business. During that period, he also found interest and entertainment in the performances of Yiddish theatre, despite the misgivings of even close friends such as Max Brod, who usually supported him in everything else. Those performances also served as a starting point for his growing relationship with Judaism.[12]

Later years

In 1912, at Max Brod's home, Kafka met Felice Bauer, who lived in Berlin and worked as a representative for a dictaphone company. Over the next five years they corresponded a great deal, met occasionally, and twice were engaged to be married. Their relationship finally ended in 1917.

In 1917, Kafka began to suffer from tuberculosis, which would require frequent convalescence during which he was supported by his family, most notably his sister Ottla. Despite his fear of being perceived as both physically and mentally repulsive, he impressed others with his boyish, neat, and austere good looks, a quiet and cool demeanor, obvious intelligence and dry sense of humor.[13]

Kafka developed an intense relationship with Czech journalist and writer Milena Jesenská. In July of 1923, throughout a vacation to Graal-Müritz on the Baltic Sea, he met Dora Diamant and briefly moved to Berlin in the hope of distancing himself from his family's influence to concentrate on his writing. In Berlin, he lived with Diamant, a 25-year-old kindergarten teacher from an orthodox Jewish family, who was independent enough to have escaped her past in the ghetto. She became his lover, and influenced Kafka's interest in the Talmud.[14]

Kafka's tuberculosis worsened in spite of using naturopathic treatments; he returned to Prague, then went to Dr. Hoffmann's sanatorium in Kierling near Vienna for treatment, where he died on 3 June 1924, apparently from starvation. The condition of Kafka's throat made eating too painful for him, and since parenteral nutrition had not yet been developed, there was no way to feed him. His body was ultimately brought back to Prague where he was buried on 11 June 1924, in the New Jewish Cemetery (sector 21, row 14, plot 33) in Prague-ikov.

Judaism and Zionism

Kafka was not formally involved in Jewish religious life, but he showed a great interest in Jewish culture and spirituality. He was well versed in Yiddish literature, and loved Yiddish theatre.[15]

In his essay, *Sadness in Palestine?!,* Dan Miron explores Kafka's connection to Zionism. "It seems that those who claim that there was such a connection and that Zionism played a central role in his life and literary work, and those who deny the connection altogether or dismiss its importance, are both wrong. The truth lies in some very elusive place between these two simplistic poles."[15]

According to James Hawes, Kafka, though much aware of his own Jewishness, did not incorporate his Jewishness into his work. "There is zero actual Jewishness" nor any Jewish characters or specifically Jewish scenes in his work, says Hawes.[16] In the opinion of literary critic Harold Bloom, author of *The Western Canon,* however, "Despite all his denials and beautiful evasions, [Kafka's writing] quite simply is Jewish writing."[12] Lothar Kahn is likewise unequivocal: "The presence of Jewishness in Kafka's *oeuvre* is no longer subject to doubt."[17] Pavel Eisner, one of Kafka's first translators, interprets the classic, *The Trial,* as the "triple dimension of Jewish existence in Prague is embodied in Kafka's *The Trial*: his protagonist Josef K. is (symbolically) arrested by a German (Rabensteiner), a Czech (Kullich), and a Jew (Kaminer). He stands for the "guiltless guilt" that imbues the Jew in the modern world, although there is no evidence that he himself is a Jew." [18]

Livia Rothkirchen calls Kafka the "symbolic figure of his era". His era included numerous other Jewish writers (Czech, German, and national Jews) who were sensitive to German, Czech, Austrian, and Jewish culture. According to Rothkirchen, "This situation lent their writings a broad cosmopolitan outlook and a quality of exaltation bordering on transcendental metaphysical contemplation. An illustrious example is Franz Kafka."[18]

Literary career

Online image: Franz Kafka's grave in Prague-ikov.

Kafka's writing attracted little attention until after his death. During his lifetime, he published only a few short stories and never finished any of his novels, unless *The Metamorphosis* is considered a (short) novel. Prior to his death, Kafka wrote to his friend and literary executor Max Brod: "Dearest Max, my last request: Everything I leave behind me ... in the way of diaries, manuscripts, letters (my own and others'), sketches, and so on, [is] to be burned unread."[19] Brod overrode Kafka's wishes, believing that Kafka had given these directions to him specifically because Kafka knew he would not honor themBrod had told him as much. (His lover, Dora Diamant, also ignored his wishes, secretly keeping up to 20 notebooks and 35 letters until they were confiscated by the Gestapo in 1933. An ongoing international search is being conducted for these missing Kafka papers.) Brod, in fact, would oversee the publication of most of Kafka's work in his possession, which soon began to attract attention and high critical regard.

All of Kafka's published works, except several letters he wrote in Czech to Milena Jesenská, were written in German.

Writing style

Kafka often made extensive use of a characteristic peculiar to the German language allowing for long sentences that sometimes can span an entire page. Kafka's sentences then deliver an unexpected impact just before the full stopthat being the finalizing meaning and focus. This is achieved due to the construction of certain sentences in German which require that the verb be positioned at the end of the sentence. Such constructions cannot be duplicated in English, so it is up to the resourceful translator to provide the reader with the same (or at least equivalent) effect found in the original text.[20]

Another virtually insurmountable problem facing the translator is how to deal with the author's intentional use of ambiguous terms or of words that have several meanings. One such instance is found in the first sentence of *The Metamorphosis*. English translators have often sought to render the word *Ungeziefer* as "insect"; in Middle German, however, *Ungeziefer* literally means "unclean animal not suitable for sacrifice"[21] and is sometimes used colloquially to mean "bug" a very general term, unlike the scientific sounding "insect". Kafka had no intention of labeling Gregor, the protagonist of the story, as any specific thing, but instead wanted to convey Gregor's disgust at his transformation. Another example is Kafka's use of the German noun *Verkehr* in the final sentence of *The Judgment*. Literally, *Verkehr* means intercourse and, as in English, can have either a sexual or non-sexual meaning; in addition, it is used to mean transport or traffic. The sentence can be translated as: "At that moment an unending stream of traffic crossed over the bridge."[22] What gives added weight to the obvious double meaning of 'Verkehr' is Kafka's confession to Max Brod that when he wrote that final line, he was thinking of "a violent ejaculation".[23]

Critical interpretations

Online image: Bronze statue of Franz Kafka in Prague.

Critics have interpreted Kafka's works in the context of a variety of literary schools, such as modernism, magic realism, and so on.[24] The apparent hopelessness and absurdity that seem to permeate his works are considered emblematic of existentialism. Others have tried to locate a Marxist influence in his satirization of bureaucracy in pieces such as *In the Penal Colony*, *The Trial*, and *The Castle*,[24] whereas others point to anarchism as an inspiration for Kafka's anti-bureaucratic viewpoint. Still others have interpreted his works through the lens of Judaism (Borges made a few perceptive remarks in this regard), through freudianism[24] (because of his familial struggles), or as allegories of a metaphysical quest for God (Thomas Mann was a proponent of this theory).[25]

Themes of alienation and persecution are repeatedly emphasized, and the emphasis on this quality, notably in the work of Marthe Robert, partly inspired the counter-criticism of Gilles Deleuze and Félix Guattari, who argued in *Kafka: Toward a Minor Literature* that there was much more to Kafka than the stereotype of a lonely figure writing out of anguish, and that his work was more deliberate, subversive, and more "joyful" than it appears to be.

Furthermore, an isolated reading of Kafka's workfocusing on the futility of his characters' struggling without the influence of any studies on Kafka's lifereveals the humor of Kafka. Kafka's work, in this sense, is not a written reflection of any of his own struggles, but a reflection of how people invent struggles.[26]

Biographers have said that it was common for Kafka to read chapters of the books he was working on to his closest friends, and that those readings usually concentrated on the humorous side of his prose. Milan Kundera refers to the essentially surrealist humour of Kafka as a main predecessor of later artists such as Federico Fellini, Gabriel García Márquez, Carlos Fuentes and Salman Rushdie. For García Márquez, it was as he said the reading of Kafka's *The Metamorphosis* that showed him "that it was possible to write in a different way."

Law in Kafka's fiction

Many attempts have been made to examine Kafkas legal background and the role of law in his fiction. These attempts remain relatively few in number compared to the vast collection of literature devoted to the study of his life and works, and marginal to legal scholarship. Mainstream studies of Kafkas works normally present his fiction as an engagement with absurdity, a critique of bureaucracy or a search for redemption, failing to account for the images of law and legality which constitute an important part of "the horizon of meaning" in his fiction. Many of his descriptions of the legal proceedings in *The Trial* metaphysical, absurd, bewildering and "Kafkaesque" as they might appear are, in fact, based on accurate and informed descriptions of German and Austrian criminal proceedings of the time. The significance of law in Kafkas fiction is also neglected within legal scholarship, for as Richard Posner pointed out, most lawyers do not consider writings about law in the form of fiction of any relevance to the understanding or the practice of law. Regardless of the concerns of mainstream studies of Kafka with redemption and absurdity, and what jurists such as Judge Posner might think relevant to law and legal practice, the fact remains that Kafka was an insurance lawyer who, besides being involved in litigation, was also "keenly aware of the legal debates of his day" (Ziolkowski, 2003, p. 224).[27]

In a recent study which uses Kafka's office writings[28] as its point of departure, Reza Banakar argues that "legal images in Kafkas fiction are worthy of examination, not only because of their bewildering, enigmatic, bizarre, profane and alienating effects, or because of the deeper theological or existential meaning they suggest, but also as a particular concept of law and legality which operates paradoxically as an integral part of the human condition under modernity[29]. To explore this point Kafkas conception of law is placed in the context of his overall writing as a search for Heimat which takes us beyond the instrumental understanding of law advocated by various schools of legal positivism and allows us to grasp law as a form of experience" (see Banakar 2010).

Publications

Much of Kafka's work was unfinished, or prepared for publication posthumously by Max Brod. The novels *The Castle* (which stopped mid-sentence and had ambiguity on content), *The Trial* (chapters were unnumbered and some were incomplete) and *Amerika* (Kafka's original title was *The Man who Disappeared*) were all prepared for publication by Brod. It appears Brod took a few liberties with the manuscript (moving chapters, changing the German and cleaning up the punctuation), and thus the original German text was altered prior to publication. The editions by Brod are generally referred to as the Definitive Editions.

According to the publisher's note[30] for *The Castle*,[31] Malcolm Pasley was able to get most of Kafka's original handwritten work into the Oxford Bodleian Library in 1961. The text for *The Trial* was later acquired through auction and is stored at the German literary archives[32] at Marbach, Germany.[33]

Subsequently, Pasley headed a team (including Gerhard Neumann, Jost Schillemeit, and Jürgen Born) in reconstructing the German novels and S. Fischer Verlag republished them.[34] Pasley was the editor for *Das Schloß (The Castle)*, published in 1982, and *Der Prozeß (The Trial)*, published in 1990. Jost Schillemeit was the editor of *Der Verschollene (Amerika)* published in 1983. These are all called the "Critical Editions" or the "Fischer Editions." The German critical text of these, and Kafka's other works, may be found online at *The Kafka Project*.[35] This site is continuously building the repository.

There is another Kafka Project based at San Diego State University, which began in 1998 as the official international search for Kafka's last writings. Consisting of 20 notebooks and 35 letters to Kafka's last companion, Dora Diamant (later, Dymant-Lask), this missing literary treasure was confiscated from her by the Gestapo in Berlin 1933. The Kafka Project's four-month search of government archives in Berlin in 1998 uncovered the confiscation order and other significant documents. In 2003, the Kafka Project discovered three original Kafka letters, written in 1923. Building on the search conducted by Max Brod and Klaus Wagenbach in the mid-1950s, the Kafka Project at SDSU has an advisory committee of international scholars and researchers, and is calling for volunteers who want to help solve a literary mystery.[36]

In 2008, academic and Kafka expert James Hawes accused scholars of suppressing details of the pornography Kafka subscribed to (published by the same man who was Kafka's own first publisher) in order to preserve his image as a quasi-saintly "outsider".[16]

Translations

There are two primary sources for the translations based on the two German editions. The earliest English translations were by Edwin and Willa Muir and published by Alfred A. Knopf. These editions were widely published and spurred the late-1940s surge in Kafka's popularity in the United States. Later editions (notably the 1954 editions) had the addition of the deleted text translated by Eithne Wilkins and Ernst Kaiser. These are known as "Definitive Editions." They translated both *The Trial, Definitive* and *The Castle, Definitive* among other writings. Definitive Editions are generally accepted to have a number of biases and to be dated in interpretation.

After Pasley and Schillemeit completed their recompilation of the German text, the new translations were completed and published *The Castle, Critical* by Mark Harman (Schocken Books, 1998), *The Trial, Critical* by Breon Mitchell (Schocken Books, 1998) and *Amerika: The Man Who Disappeared* by Michael Hoffman (New Directions Publishing, 2004). These editions are often noted as being based on the restored text.

Published works

See also: Franz Kafka bibliography

Short stories

- *Description of a Struggle* (*Beschreibung eines Kampfes*, 19041905)
- *Wedding Preparations in the Country* (*Hochzeitsvorbereitungen auf dem Lande*, 19071908)
- *Contemplation* (Betrachtung, 19041912)
- *The Judgment* (*Das Urteil*, 2223 September 1912)
- *The Stoker*
- *In the Penal Colony* (*In der Strafkolonie*, October 1914)
- *The Village Schoolmaster* (*Der Dorfschullehrer* or *Der Riesenmaulwurf*, 19141915)
- *Blumfeld, an Elderly Bachelor* (*Blumfeld, ein älterer Junggeselle*, 1915)
- *The Warden of the Tomb* (*Der Gruftwächter*, 19161917), the only play Kafka wrote
- *The Hunter Gracchus* (*Der Jäger Gracchus*, 1917)
- *The Great Wall of China* (*Beim Bau der Chinesischen Mauer*, 1917)
- *A Report to an Academy* (*Ein Bericht für eine Akademie*, 1917)

- *Jackals and Arabs (Schakale und Araber,* 1917)
- *A Country Doctor (Ein Landarzt,* 1919)
- *A Message from the Emperor (Eine kaiserliche Botschaft,* 1919)
- *An Old Manuscript (Ein altes Blatt,* 1919)
- *The Refusal (Die Abweisung,* 1920)
- *A Hunger Artist (Ein Hungerkünstler,* 1924)
- *Investigations of a Dog (Forschungen eines Hundes,* 1922)
- *A Little Woman (Eine kleine Frau,* 1923)
- *First Sorrow (Erstes Leid,* 19211922)
- *The Burrow (Der Bau,* 19231924)
- *Josephine the Singer, or the Mouse Folk (Josephine, die Sängerin, oder Das Volk der Mäuse,* 1924)

Many collections of the stories have been published, and they include:

- *The Penal Colony: Stories and Short Pieces.* New York: Schocken Books, 1948.
- *The Complete Stories,* (ed. Nahum N. Glatzer). New York: Schocken Books, 1971.
- *The Basic Kafka.* New York: Pocket Books, 1979.
- *The Sons.* New York: Schocken Books, 1989.
- *The Metamorphosis, In the Penal Colony, and Other Stories.* New York: Schocken Books, 1995.
- *Contemplation.* Twisted Spoon Press, 1998.
- *Metamorphosis and Other Stories.* Penguin Classics, 2007

Novellas

- *The Metamorphosis (Die Verwandlung,* November December 1915)

Novels

- *The Trial (Der Prozeß,* 1925) (includes short story Before the Law)
- *The Castle (Das Schloß,* 1926)
- *Amerika (Amerika* or *Der Verschollene,* 1927)

Diaries and notebooks

- *Diaries 19101923*
- *The Blue Octavo Notebooks*

Letters

- *Letter to His Father*
- *Letters to Felice*
- *Letters to Ottla*
- *Letters to Milena*
- *Letters to Family, Friends, and Editors*

Commemoration

Online image: The entrance to the Franz Kafka museum in Prague.

Franz Kafka has a museum dedicated to his work in Prague, Czech Republic.

The term "Kafkaesque" is widely used to describe concepts, situations, and ideas which are reminiscent of Kafka's works, particularly *The Trial* and *The Metamorphosis*.

In Mexico, the phrase "Si Franz Kafka fuera mexicano, sería costumbrista" (If Franz Kafka were Mexican, he would be a Costumbrista writer) is commonly used in newspapers, blogs, and online forums to tell how hopeless and absurd the situation in the country is.[37]

It has been noted that "from the Czech point of view, Kafka was German, and from the German point of view he was, above all, Jewish" and that this was a common "fate of much of Western Jewry."[11]

Literary and cultural references (URLs online)

Literature

- Nobel Prize winner Isaac Bashevis Singer wrote a short story called "A Friend of Kafka," which was about a Yiddish actor called Jacques Kohn who said he knew Franz Kafka. In this story, according to Jacques Kohn, Kafka believed in the Golem, a legendary creature from Jewish folklore.[38]
- *Kafka Americana* by Jonathan Lethem and Carter Scholz is a collection of stories based on Kafka's life and works.
- *Kafka on the Shore* by Haruki Murakami
- *Kafka was the Rage, a Greenwich Village Memoir* by Anatole Broyard
- *Kafka's Curse* by Achmat Dangor
- *The Kafka Effekt* by American bizarro author D. Harlan Wilson, who relates his take on the irrealism genre of literature to that of Franz Kafka, and to that of William S. Burroughs.
- *Criminal (comics)* by Ed Brubaker and Sean Phillips contains, within a re-occurring comic strip seen in characters newspapers, the adventures of 'Franz Kafka PI'. The 4th story arc of the book also involves the creator of the strip. There is talk of a spin off series written by Matt Fraction.

Short stories

- Zoetrope an experimental avant-garde short film by Charlie Deaux, *Zoetrope (1999)* at the Internet Movie Database. Adaptation of "In the Penal Colony".
- *The Hunger Artist (2002)* at the Internet Movie Database an animated feature by Tom Gibbons

- *Menschenkörper (2004)* at the Internet Movie Database[39] Adaptation of "A Country Doctor". Short film by Tobias Frühmorgen
- *A Country Doctor (2007)* at the Internet Movie Database Adaptation of "A Country Doctor". Short film by Koji Yamamura
- Science Fiction author Rudy Rucker has published a short story titled "The 57th Franz Kafka", which is also the title of a collection of his short stories.

Film and Television

- *Kafka* (1990) Jeremy Irons stars as the eponymous author. Written by Lem Dobbs and directed by Steven Soderbergh, the movie mixes his life and fiction providing a semi-biographical presentation of Kafka's life and works. The story concerns Kafka investigating the disappearance of one of his work colleagues. The plot takes Kafka through many of the writer's own works, most notably *The Castle* and *The Trial*.
- *Franz Kafka (1992)* at the Internet Movie Database an animated film by Piotr Dumaa
- *The Trial* (1962) Orson Welles wrote and directed this adaptation of the novel starring Anthony Perkins, Jeanne Moreau, and Romy Schneider. In a 1962 BBC Interview with Huw Wheldon, Orson Welles noted, "Say what you like, but *The Trial* is the best film I have ever made".
- *Klassenverhältnisse Class Relations* (1984) Directed by the experimental filmmaking duo of Jean-Marie Straub and Danièle Huillet based on Kafka's novel *Amerika*.
- *The Trial* (1993) Starring Kyle MacLachlan as Joseph K. with Anthony Hopkins in a cameo role as the priest as a strictly faithful adaptation with a screenplay by playwright Harold Pinter.
- A Movie Adaptation of (The Castle) *Das Schloß (1997)* at the Internet Movie Database by Michael Haneke. More on Das Schloß (film)
- The character Daria in MTV's *Daria* has a poster of Kafka in her bedroom. Seventeen Magazine wrote an article about Daria's bedroom and mentions the poster. *Seventeen asks Daria if existentialist author Franz Kafka is her hero. She replies, "The guy writes a novella about a man turning into a cockroach, and you have to ask if he's a hero?"*
- In an episode of Adult Swim's *Home Movies (TV series)*, Duane of the rock group Scab wrote a rock opera about the life of Franz Kafka and played the title character.
- Suda51 is planning to make a game based on *The Castle* entitled "Kurayami".
- *Kafka goes to the Forest* (2009) a short experimental film directed by Daniel Matos, the movie is a surreal representation of his last days internal conflicts.

Metamorphosis

- *Die Verwandlung* at the Internet Movie Database
- *Förvandlingen* at the Internet Movie Database
- *The Metamorphosis of Mr. Samsa* at the Internet Movie Database, an animated short by Caroline Leaf
- *Metamorphosis* at the Internet Movie Database
- *Franz Kafka's 'It's a Wonderful Life'* (1993) is an Oscar-winning short film written and directed by Peter Capaldi and starring Richard E. Grant as Kafka. The film blends *The Metamorphosis* with Frank Capra's *It's a Wonderful Life*.
- *The Metamorphosis of Franz Kafka (1993)* by Carlos Atanes.

- *Prevrashcheniye* at the Internet Movie Database
- *Metamorfosis* at the Internet Movie Database

Theatre

- Alan Bennett, *Kafka's Dick*, 1986, a play in which the ghosts of Kafka, his father Hermann, and Max Brod arrive at the home of an English insurance clerk (and Kafka aficionado) and his wife.
- Milan Richter, *Kafka's Hell-Paradise*, 2006, a play with 5 characters, using Kafka's aphorisms, dreams and re-telling his relations to his father and to the women. Translated from the Slovak by Ewald Osers.
- Milan Richter, *Kafka's Second Life*, 2007, a play with 17 characters, starting in Kierling where Kafka is dying and ending in Prague in 1961. Translated from the Slovak by Ewald Osers.
- Tadeusz Róewicz, *Puapka (The Trap)*, 1982, a play loosely based on Kafka's diaries and letters

Music

- Hungarian composer György Kurtág wrote a piece for soprano and violin, using fragments of Kafka's diary and letters: *Kafka-Fragmente*, Op. 24, 1985.
- Russian hip hop band 2H Company refers to *The Metamorphosis* in their probably most famous song "Adaptation". The main hero of the song read the novella before going to bed, and then had a dream that caused all humans' bodies transformation.
- Australian band Lost Valentinos released their song "Kafka" on a 2005 EP release titled "The Valentinos". The track "Kafka" uses imparted knowledge of Kafka's death as a symbolism of frustration and desperate helplessness in the downfall of a relationship.
- In the song "Eleven Saints" by Jason Webley Kafka is metioned in the lyrics, "...we're just sittin' by the train tracks reading Kafka to the sky,".
- Josef Tals last opera Josef (1993), is inspired in part by Franz Kafka Josef Tal In Memoriam

See also (online edition)

- Asteroid 3412 Kafka, named after the author.
- Franz Kafka Prize

References (URLs online)

- 1. Franz Kafka Franz Kafka
- 2. (Spanish)Contijoch, Francesc Miralles (2000) "Franz Kafka". *Oceano Grupo Editorial, S.A. Barcelona.* ISBN 84-494-1811-9.
- 3. Corngold 1973
- 4. Gilman, Sander L. (2005) *Franz Kafka.* Reaktion Books Ltd. London, UK. p. 2021. ISBN 1-88187-264-5.
- 5. Hamalian ([1975], 3).

- 6. Danuta Czech: Kalendarz wydarze w KL Auschwitz, Owicim 1992, p. 534. In the archives of the camp a list with the names of the guardians was preserved.
- 7. Derek Sayer, "The language of nationality and the nationality of language: Prague 17801920 Czech Republic history", Past and Present, 1996; 153: 164210.
- 8. Letter to his Father, p. 150
- 9. *Lambent Traces: Franz Kafka* S Corngold - 2004
- 10. Drucker, Peter. Managing in the Next Society. See: Franz Kafka, *Amtliche Schriften*. Eds. K. Hermsdorf & B. Wagner (2004) (Engl. transl.: *The Office Writings*. Eds. S. Corngold, J. Greenberg & B. Wagner. Transl. E. Patton with R. Hein (2008)); cf. H.-G. Koch & K. Wagenbach (eds.), *Kafkas Fabriken* (2002).
- 11. *The Metamorphosis and Other Stories*, notes. Herberth Czermak. Lincoln, Nebraska: Cliffs Notes 1973, 1996.
- 12. "Kafka and Judaism". Victorian.fortunecity.com. Retrieved 28 May 2009.
- 13. Ryan McKittrick speaks with director Dominique Serrand and Gideon Lester about *Amerika* www.amrep.org
- 14. Lothar Hempel www.atlegerhardsen.com
- 15. "Sadness in Palestine". Haaretz.com. Retrieved 28 May 2009.
- 16. Franz Kafkas porn brought out of the closet - Times Online at entertainment.timesonline.co.uk
- 17. Lothar Kahn, in *Between Two Worlds: a cultural history of German-Jewish writers,* page 191
- 18. Livia Rothkirchen, *The Jews of Bohemia and Moravia: facing the Holocaust*, University of Nebraska Press, 2005 p. 23
- 19. Quoted in Publisher's Note to *The Castle*, Schocken Books.
- 20. Kafka (1996, xi).
- 21. ungeziefer Dictionary / Wörterbuch (BEOLINGUS, TU Chemnitz)
- 22. Kafka (1996, 75).
- 23. Brod. Max: "Franz Kafka, a Biography". (trans. Humphreys Roberts) New York: Schocken Books,1960. p. 129.
- 24. Franz Kafka 1883 1924 www.coskunfineart.com
- 25. *Thomas Mann, the ironic German.* E Heller, T Mann - 1981
- 26. *Franz Kafka* (1883-1924)nih.gov.D Felisati, G Sperati - Acta Otorhinolaryngologica Italica, 2005 - ncbi.nlm.nih.gov
- 27. For an overview of studies which focus on Kafkas images of law see Banakar, Reza. "In Search of Heimat: A Note on Franz Kafka's Concept of Law". Forthcoming in Law and Literature 2010. An e-copy available at http://papers.ssrn.com/sol3/papers.cfm?abstract_id=1574870
- 28. Corngold, Stanley et. al., (eds.) Franz Kafka: The Office Writings. Princeton, Princeton University Press, 2009.
- 29. "In Search of Heimat: A Note on Franz Kafka's Concept of Law" at http://papers.ssrn.com/sol3/papers.cfm?abstract_id=1574870
- 30. A Kafka For The 21st century by Arthur Samuelson, publisher, Schocken Books www.jhom.com
- 31. Schocken Books, 1998
- 32. (German) Herzlich Willkommen www.dla-marbach.de
- 33. (publisher's note, *The Trial*, Schocken Books, 1998
- 34. *Stepping into Kafkas head*, Jeremy Adler, Times Literary Supplement, 13 October 1995 <http://www.textkritik.de/rezensionen/kafka/einl_04.htm⟩

○ 35. The Kafka Project all Kafka text in German According to the Manuscript www.kafka.org

○ 36. Sources: Kafka, by Nicolas Murray, pages 367, 374; Kafka's Last Love, by Kathi Diamant; "Summary of the Results of the Kafka Project Berlin Research 1 June September 1998" published in December 1998 Kafka Katern, quarterly of the Kafka Circle of the Netherlands. More information is available at http://www.kafkaproject.com

○ 37. Aquella, Daniel (22 November 2006). "México kafkiano y costumbrista". *Daquella manera:Paseo personal por inquietudes culturales, sociales y lo que tengamos a bien obrar.*. Retrieved 16 February 2007.

○ 38. Bashevis Singer, Isaac (1970). *A Friend of Kafka, and Other Stories*. Farrar, Straus and Giroux. p. 311. ISBN 0-37415-880-0.

○ 39. (German) Menschenkörper movie website www.menschenkoerper.de

Bibliography

○ Adorno, Theodor. *Prisms*. Cambridge: The MIT Press, 1967.

○ Banakar, Reza. "In Search of Heimat: A Note on Franz Kafka's Concept of Law". Forthcoming in Law and Literature volume 22, 2010. [1]

○ Corngold, Stanley. *Introduction to The Metamorphosis*. Bantam Classics, 1972. ISBN 0-553-21369-5.

○ Hamalian, Leo, ed. *Franz Kafka: A Collection of Criticism*. New York: McGraw-Hill, 1974. ISBN 0-07-025702-7.

○ Heller, Paul. *Franz Kafka: Wissenschaft und Wissenschaftskritik*. Tuebingen: Stauffenburg, 1989. ISBN 3-923-72140-4.

○ Kafka, Franz. *The Metamorphosis and Other Stories*. Trans. Donna Freed. New York: Barnes & Noble, 1996. ISBN 1-56619-969-7.

○ Kafka, Franz. *Kafka's Selected Stories*. Norton Critical Edition. Trans. Stanley Corngold. New York: Norton, 2005. ISBN 9780393924794.

○ Brod, Max. *Franz Kafka: A Biography*. New York: Da Capo Press, 1995. ISBN 0-306-80670-3

○ Brod, Max. *The Biography of Franz Kafka*, tr. from the German by G. Humphreys Roberts. London: Secker & Warburg, 1947. OCLC 2771397

○ Calasso, Roberto. *K*. Knopf, 2005. ISBN 1-4000-4189-9

○ Citati, Pietro, *Kafka*, 1987. ISBN 0-7859-2173-7

○ Coots, Steve. *Franz Kafka (Beginner's Guide)*. Headway, 2002, ISBN 0-340-84648-8

○ Deleuze, Gilles & Félix Guattari. *Kafka: Toward a Minor Literature (Theory and History of Literature, Vol 30)*. Minneapolis, University of Minnesota, 1986. ISBN 0-8166-1515-2

○ Danta, Chris. "Sarah's Laughter: Kafka's Abraham" in *Modernism/Modernity* 15:2 ([2] April 2008), 34359.

○ Glatzer, Nahum N., *The Loves of Franz Kafka*. New York: Schocken Books, 1986. ISBN 0-8052-4001-2

○ Greenberg, Martin, *The Terror of Art: Kafka and Modern Literature*. New York, Basic Books, 1968. ISBN 0-465-08415-X

○ Gordimer, Nadine (1984). "Letter from His Father" in *Something Out There*, London, Penguin Books. ISBN 0-14-007711-1 o Hayman, Ronald. *K, a Biography of Kafka*. London: Phoenix Press, 2001.ISBN 1-84212-415-3

o Janouch, Gustav. *Conversations with Kafka*. New York: New Directions Books, second edition 1971. (Translated by Goronwy Rees.)ISBN 0-8112-0071-X

o Murray, Nicholas. *Kafka*. New Haven: Yale, 2004.

o Pawel, Ernst. *The Nightmare of Reason: A Life of Franz Kafka*. New York: Vintage Books, 1985. ISBN 0-374-52335-5

o Thiher, Allen (ed.). *Franz Kafka: A Study of the Short Fiction* (Twayne's Studies in Short Fiction, No. 12). ISBN 0-8057-8323-7

o Philippe Zard: *La fiction de l'Occident Thomas Mann, Franz Kafka, Albert Cohen*, Paris, P.U.F., 1999.

o Philippe Zard (ed) *Sillage de Kafka*, Paris, Le Manuscrit, 2007, ISBN 2-7481-8610-9.

o Ziolkowski, Theodore, The Mirror of Justice: Literary Reflections of Legal Crisis. Princeton, Princeton University Press, 2003 (first ed. 1997)

Websites (URLs online)

o Franz Kafka in the German National Library catalogue (German)
o Works by Franz Kafka at Project Gutenberg
o Franz Kafka at the Internet Movie Database
o Kafka-metamorphosis public wiki dedicated to Kafka and his work
o The Kafka Project project to publish online all Kafka texts in German
o End of Kafkaesque nightmare: writer's papers finally come to light
o Kafka Society of America
o Deutsche Kafka-Gesellschaft
o Spolecnost Franze Kafky a nakladatelstvi Franze Kafky Franz Kafka Society and Publishing House in Prague
o Oxford Kafka Research Centre information on ongoing international Kafka research
o Journeys of Franz Kafka Photographs of places where Kafka lived and worked
o Finding Kafka in Prague Trying to find Kafka in today's Prague

A hyperlinked version of this chapter is at http://booksllc.net?q=Franz%5FKafka

10

FRANZ KARL GINZKEY

Franz Karl Ginzkey (September 8, 1871, Pola, Austrian Littoral, Austria-Hungary (now Pula, Croatia) - April 11, 1963, Seewalchen am Attersee, Upper Austria, Austria) was an austro-Hungarian (then Austrian) officer, poet and writer. His arguably most famous book *Hatschi Bratschis Luftballon* (*Hatschi Bratschis balloon*) captivated generations of children.

Life

Franz Karl Ginzkey, son of a Sudeten German professional officer of the Austrian Navy, was in the imperial army until 1897. During that period he was intermittently also commander of the as barracks used (Rainer-infantry regiment) Fortress Hohensalzburg. From 1897 to 1914 he worked as a cartographer at the *Militärgeographischen Institute* (*Militarygeographic institute*) in Vienna, afterwards in the war archive. Since 1920, he was a retired military member and then worked as a freelance writer. At the time of the Austro-Fascism, he was (for the professional group of artists) from 1934 to 1938 Member of the Council of State and after 1938 came to terms with the leaders of National Socialism. He was friends with Max Mell and Stefan Zweig, and furthermore with Faistauer Anton and Carl Zuckmayer. Moreover, Ginzkey participated in the founding of the Salzburg Festival and for decades was a member of its board of trustees. Since 1944 he lived in Seewalchen at Lake Attersee.

After the end of war Ginzkeys *Die Front in Tirol* (*The front in Tyrol*) (Fischer, Berlin, 1916) was blacklisted in the Soviet zone of occupation. [1]

On his 100th birthday a *Franz-Karl-Ginzkey* monument was erected in Seewalchen at Lake Attersee.

He rests in a grave of honor at the Vienna Central Cemetery (Group 32 C, Number 25).

Ginzkey is numbered among the circle of *newromantic* poets and novelists. One of his literary discoverers was Peter Rosegger. A part of his work shows great connection to Salzburg. This witness the following works:

* Wie ich Herr auf Hohensalzburg ward *When I was master at Hohensalzburg*
Altsalzburger Bilder nach 10 Federzeichnungen (gemeinsam mit Ulf Seidl)
Altsalzburger images after 10 pen drawings (together with Ulf Seidl)
Jakobus und die Frauen (1908) *Jacob and the Women*
Der seltsame Soldat (1925) *The strange soldier*
Der Heimatsucher (1948) *The home searcher*
Das Antlitz Salzburgs (1933) *The face of Salzburg*
Salzburg und das Salzkammergut (1934) *Salzburg and the Salzkammergut*
Prinz Tunora (1934) *Prince Tunora*
Salzburg, sein Volk und seine Trachten (1934) *Salzburg, its people and its costumes*

In 1968 the square between *Alpenstraße* (*Alpine street*) and *Adolf-Schemel-Straße* (*Adolf-Schemel street*) in the Salzburg district of *Salzburg-Süd* (*Salzburg-South*) (Alpinsiedlung) was named in his honor *Ginzkeyplatz*.

Literary works (a selection)

- *Hatschi Bratschis Luftballon*, 1904
- *Der von der Vogelweide*, 1912
- *Der Wiesenzaun. Erzählung*, 1913
- *Aus der Werkstatt des Lyrikers. Vortrag*, 1913
- *Den Herren Feinden! Ein Trutz- und Mahnlied*, 1914
- *Die Front in Tirol*, 1916
- *Der Gaukler von Bologna*, Roman, 1916
- *Befreite Stunde. Neue Gedichte*, 1917
- *Der Doppelspiegel. Betrachtungen und Erzählungen*, 1920
- *Rositta*, 1921
- *Der Prinz von Capestrano*, 1921

- *Von wunderlichen Wegen. 7 Erzählungen*, 1922
- *Brigitte und Regine*, Novelle, 1923
- *Die Reise nach Komakuku. Geschichten aus seltsamer Jugend*, 1923
- *Der Weg zu Oswalda. Erählung*, 1924
- *Der seltsame Soldat*, 1925
- *Der Kater Ypsilon. Novellen*, 1926
- *Der Gott und die Schauspielerin*, 1928
- *Florians wundersame Reise über die Tapete*, 1931
- *Drei Frauen. Rosita - Agnete - Oswalda*, 1931
- *Gespenster auf Hirschberg. Aus der hinterlassenen Handschrift des Majors von Baltram*, 1931
- *Das verlorene Herz. Ein Märchenspiel*, 1931
- *Magie des Schicksals. Novelle*, 1932
- *Das Antlitz Salzburgs*, 1933
- *Prinz Tunora*, Roman, 1934
- *Salzburg und das Salzkammergut*, 1934
- *Salzburg, sein Volk und seine Trachten*, 1934
- *Liselotte und ihr Ritter oder Warum nicht Romantik?*, Roman, 1936
- *Sternengast. Neue Gedichte*, 1937
- *Der selige Brunnen. Eine Raphael Donner-Novelle*, 1940
- *Meistererzählungen*, 1940
- *Erschaffung der Eva. Ein epischer Gesang*, 1941
- *Zeit und Menschen meiner Jugend*, 1942
- *Taniwani. Ein fröhliches Fischbuch*, 1947
- *Der Heimatsucher. Ein Leben und eine Sehnsucht*, 1948
- *Genius Mozart*, 1949
- *Die Geschichte einer stillen Frau*, Roman, 1951
- *Der Träumerhansl*, 1952
- *Altwiener Balladen*, 1955
- *Der Tanz auf einem Bein. Ein Seitensprung ins Wunderliche*, 1956
- *Franz Karl Ginzkey. Ausgewählte Werke in vier Bänden*, 1960

Websites (URLs online)

(all in German)

- Franz Karl Ginzkey in the German National Library catalogue (German)
- Kurzbiografie zu Franz Karl Ginzkey
- Franz Karl Ginzkey In: Projekt Historischer Roman. Datenbank. Universität Innsbruck.
- Nachlass von Franz Karl Ginzkey in der Wiener Stadt- und Landesbibliothek
- Franz-Karl-Ginzkey-Denkmal in Seewalchen am Attersee

A hyperlinked version of this chapter is at http://booksllc.net?q=Franz%5FKarl%5FGinzkey

11

GREGOR VON REZZORI

Gregor von Rezzori (born **Gregor Arnulph Hilarius d'Arezzo**; May 13, 1914
- April 23, 1998) was an Austrian-born German-language novelist, memoirist,
screenwriter and author of radio plays, as well as an actor, journalist, visual
artist, art critic and art collector. He was fluent in German, Romanian, Italian,
Polish, Russian, Yiddish, French, and English; during his life, von Rezzori was
successively a citizen of Austria-Hungary, Romania, and the Soviet Union, before
becoming a stateless person and spending his final years as a citizen of Austria.
He married Beatrice Monti della Corte.

Biography

He was born in Czernowitz, Bukovina, part of Austria-Hungary at the time. He
originated in a Sicilian aristocratic family from the Province of Ragusa, who had
settled in Vienna by the mid-1700s. His father was an Austrian civil servant based
in Czernowitz. The family remained in the region after it became part of the
Romanian Kingdom, and Gregor von Rezzori obtained Romanian citizenship.

After World War I, von Rezzori studied in colleges in Braov, Fürstenfeld and Vienna. He began studying mining at the University of Leoben, then architecture and medicine at the University of Vienna, where he eventually graduated in arts.

In mid-1930 he moved to Bucharest, took up military service in the Romanian Army, and made a living as an artist. In 1938 he moved to Berlin, where he became active as a novelist, journalist, writer in radio broadcasting, and film production. Given his Romanian citizenship, von Rezzori was not drafted by Nazi authorities during World War II.

Until the mid-1950s, he worked as an author at the broadcast company Nordwest-deutscher Rundfunk. He regularly published novels and stories, as well as being engaged in film production as a screenplay author and actor (starring alongside actors such as Brigitte Bardot, Jeanne Moreau, Anna Karina, Marcello Mastroianni or Charles Aznavour). Beginning in the early 1960s, Rezzori lived between Rome and Paris, with sojourns in the United States, eventually settling in Tuscany.

Besides authoring and performing, he and his spouse Beatrice Monti della Corte were significant art collectors, and together founded the Santa Maddalena Retreat for Writers. He died in Santa Maddalena, part of Florence's Donnini *frazione*.

Literary works

Rezzori began his career as a writer of light novels, but he first encountered success in 1953 with the *Maghrebinian Tales*, a suite of droll stories and anecdotes from an imaginary land called "Maghrebinia", which reunited in a grotesque and parodic key traits of his multicultural Bukovinian birthplace, of extinct Austria-Hungary and of Bucharest of his youth. Over the years, Rezzori published further *Maghrebinian Tales*, which increased his reputation of language virtuosity and free spirit, writing with wit, insight and elegance.[1]

Other books, such as *The Death of My Brother Abel*, *Oedipus at Stalingrad*, or *The Snows of Yesteryear*, recording the fading world at the time of the World Wars, have been celebrated for their powerful descriptive prose, nuance and style.[2]

Von Rezzori first came to the attention of English-speaking readers with the 1969 publication of the story "Memoirs of an Anti-Semite," in *The New Yorker.* On this occasion, Elie Wiesel, who was born in Bukovina's neighboring Maramure, wrote:

"Rezzori addresses the major problems of our time, and his voice echoes with the disturbing and wonderful magic of a true storyteller."[3]

In his *Guide for Idiots through the German Society*, von Rezzori also used his noted taste for satire. Although he was not unanimously perceived as a major author in the German-speaking area, his posthumous reception has arguably confirmed him among the most important modern German-language authors.[2]

Published titles

- *Flamme, die sich verzehrt* ("Self-extinguishing Flame", novel, 1940)
- *Rombachs einsame Jahre*, ("Rombach's Lonely Years", novel, 1942)
- *Rose Manzani* (novel, 1944)
- *Maghrebinische Geschichten* ("Tales of Maghrebinia", 1953)
- *Ödipus siegt bei Stalingrad* ("Oedipus at Stalingrad", 1954)
- *Männerfibel*, 1955
- *Ein Hermelin in Tschernopol. Ein maghrebinischer Roman* ("The Hussar", 1958)
- *Bogdan im Knoblauchwald. Ein maghrebinisches Märchen* ("Bogdan in the Garlic Forest. A Maghrebinian Tale", 1962)
- *Die Toten auf ihre Plätze. Tagebuch des Films Viva Maria* ("The Dead on their Places. Journal of the Movie 'Viva Maria'", 1966)
- *1001 Jahr Maghrebinien. Eine Festschrift* (1967)
- *Der Tod meines Bruders Abel* ("The Death of My Brother Abel", novel, 1976)
- *Greif zur Geige, Frau Vergangenheit* (novel, 1978)
- *Denkwürdigkeiten eines Antisemiten* ("The Memoirs of an Anti-Semite", 1979)
- *Der arbeitslose König. Maghrebinisches Märchen* ("The Jobless King. A Maghrebinian Tale", 1981)
- *A Stranger in Lolitaland. An Essay*, first published in English by *Vanity Fair*
- *Blumen im Schnee Portraitstudien zu einer Autobiographie, die ich nie schreiben werde. Auch: Versuch der Erzählweise eines gleicherweise nie geschriebenen Bildungsromans* ("The Snows Of Yesteryear", autobiographical essays, 1989)
- *Über dem Kliff* ("Beyond the Cliff", stories, 1991)
- *Idiotenführer durch die Deutsche Gesellschaft. Hochadel, Adel, Schickeria, Prominenz* ("Guide for Idiots through the German Society. Aristocracy, Swells, Notables", 1992)
- *Begegnungen* ("Encounters", 1992)
- *Greisengemurmel. Ein Rechenschaftsbericht* (1994)
- *Italien, Vaterland der Legenden, Mutterland der Mythen. Reisen durch die europäischen Vaterländer oder wie althergebrachte Gemeinplätze durch neue zu ersetzen sind* (1996)
- *Frankreich. Gottesland der Frauen und der Phrasen. Reisen durch die europäischen Vaterländer oder wie althergebrachte Gemeinplätze durch neue zu ersetzen sind* (1997)
- *Mir auf der Spur* ("On My Own Traces", 1997)
- *Kain. Das letzte Manuskript* (posthumous novel, 2001)

Awards

- Theodor-Fontane-Preis (1959)
- Premio Scanno (1987)
- Premio Boccaccio
- Premio Lorenzo Il Magnifico

Filmography

Screenwriter

- *Kopfjäger von Borneo*, 1936
- *Unter den Sternen von Capri*, 1953
- *Labyrinth*, 1959
- *The Dear Augustin*, 1959
- *Sturm im Wasserglas*, 1960
- *Man nennt es Amore* , 1961
- *Geliebte Hochstaplerin*, 1961
- *Die Herren*, 1965
- *Mord und Totschlag*, 1967

Actor

- *Sie*, 1954. Directed by Rolf Thiele, with Marina Vlady, Walter Giller, Nadja Tiller
- *El Hakim*, 1957. Directed by Rolf Thiele, with O.W. Fischer, Michael Ande, Nadja Tiller
- *Paprika*, 1959. Directed by Kurt Wilhelm with Willy Hagara, Violetta Ferrari
- *Labyrinth*, 1959. Directed by Rolf Thiele, with Nadja Tiller, Peter van Eyck, Amedeo Nazzari
- *Bezaubernde Arabella*, 1959. Directed by Axel von Ambesser, with Johanna von Koczian, Carlos Thompson, Hilde Hildebrand
- *Das Riesenrad*, 1961. Directed by Géza von Radványi, with Maria Schell, O.W. Fischer, Adrienne Gessner
- *Destination Rome*, 1962. Directed by Denys de La Patellière, with Arletty, Charles Aznavour, Monique Bert
- *A Very Private Affair*, 1962. Directed by Louis Malle, with Brigitte Bardot, Marcello Mastroianni
- *Games of Desire*, 1964. Directed by Hans Albin and Peter Berneis, with Claudine Auger, Cecilie Gelers
- *Un mari à un prix fixe*, 1965. Directed by Claude de Givray, with Anna Karina, Roger Hanin
- *Viva Maria!*, 1965. Directed by Louis Malle, and Jean-Claude Carrière, with Brigitte Bardot, Jeanne Moreau
- *Man on Horseback*, 1969. Directed by Volker Schlöndorff, with David Warner, Anna Karina
- *Ein Bißchen Liebe*, 1974. Directed by Veith von Fürstenberg, with Brigitte Berger, Eva Maria Herzig
- *Le beau monde*, 1981. Directed by Michel Polac, with Fabrice Luchini, Judith Magre

Further Reading

- Valentina Glajar: *After Empire: 'Postcolonial' Bukovina in Gregor von Rezzori's 'Blumen im Schnee' (1989)* . In: The German Legacy in East Central Europe as Recorded in Recent German-Language Literature. Columbia, SC: Camden House. 2004. ISBN 1-57113-256-2

- Katarzyna Jatal, *Erzählte Zeiträume. Kindheitserinnerungen aus den Randgebieten der Habsburgermonarchie von Manès Sperber, Elias Canetti und Gregor von Rezzori*, Aureus, Kraków, 1998
- Gerhard Köpf, *Vor-Bilder. Tübinger Poetik-Vorlesung*, Konkursbuchverlag, Tübingen, 1999
- Jacques Lajarrige, *Gregor von Rezzori. Etudes réunies*, Université de Rouen, Centre d'Études et de Recherches Autrichiennes, Mont-Saint-Aignan, 2003
- Gilbert Ravy, "Rezzori et la France", in *Austriaca*, No. 54 (2002), p.41-58

Notes

- 1. Killy, p. 410
- 2. Kraft, p.10271029
- 3. Wiesel, in *MIT Tech Talk*

References (URLs online)

- "Gregor von Rezzori at Institute as writer-in-residence; will speak Nov. 21", in *MIT Tech Talk*, Vol 41, Nr 12, November 20, 1996
- W. Killy (ed.), *Literaturlexikon*, vol. 9, Lexikon Verlag, 2001
- Th. Kraft (ed.), *Lexikon der deutschsprachigen Gegenwartsliteratur seit 1945*, Nymphenburger, Munich, 2003

Websites (URLs online)

- Gregor von Rezzori at the Internet Movie Database
- Santa Maddalena Foundation
- Review of *Orient-Express*
- Review of *Memoirs of an Anti-Semite*

A hyperlinked version of this chapter is at http://booksllc.net?q=Gregor%5Fvon%5FRezzori

12

HEIMITO VON DODERER

Heimito von Doderer (5 September 1896, in Weidlingau (now a part of Hadersdorf-Weidlingau, Penzing), near Vienna - 23 December 1966, Vienna) was a famous Austrian writer.

Life and work

Heimito von Doderer was born near Vienna in 1896, son of the architect and engineer **Wilhelm Carl von Doderer** and his wife **Wilhelmine von Hügel** as the youngest of 6 children. His unusual first name was based on an attempt to germanicize the Spanish name *"Jaime"*, or rather its diminutive *"Jaimito"*.

His life was spent mostly in Vienna, the longest exception being a period as a Russian prisoner of war in Siberia from 1916 until his eventual return to Austria in 1920. It was during his time in Russia that he decided to become a writer. His first published work, a book of poems *Gassen und Landschaft*, appeared in 1923, followed by the novel *Die Bresche* the following year, both with little success. A further novel, *Das Geheimnis des Reichs*, followed in 1930. In the same year he married **Gusti Hasterlik**, but they separated 2 years later and were divorced in 1938.

In 1933 Doderer joined the Austrian section of the NSDAP and published several stories in the *Deutschösterreichische Tages-Zeitung* ("German-Austrian Journal"), a newspaper closely linked to the party and propagating racism and the unification of Germany and Austria. In 1936 he moved to Dachau (Germany), where he met his future 2nd wife, **Emma Maria Thoma** (although they were not to marry until 1952). In Germany, he renewed his NSDAP-membership (the Austrian Nazi Party had been banned since 1933). He returned to Vienna in 1938, sharing a flat with the celebrated painter Albert Paris Gütersloh. In that year the novel *Ein Mord den jeder begeht* was published. His conversion to catholicism in 1940 was the result of the distance to the Nazi party which had grown over the past years, and of his reading of Thomas Aquinas. In this year, he was called up to the Wehrmacht and was later posted to France, where he began work on his most celebrated novel *Die Strudlhofstiege*. Due to ill health, he was allowed in 1943 to return from the front, serving in the Vienna area, before a final posting to Oslo at the end of the war.

After his return to Austria in early 1946 he was banned from publishing. This ban was lifted in 1947. He continued work on *Die Strudlhofstiege*, but although he completed it in 1948, the still obscure author was unable to get it published immediately. However when it did finally appear in 1951 it was a huge success, and its author's place in the post-war Austrian literary scene was assured. After this he returned to an earlier unfinished project, *Die Dämonen*, which appeared in 1956 to much acclaim. In 1958 he began work on what was intended to be a four volume novel under the general title of "Novel No. 7", to be written as a counterpart to Beethoven's 7th Symphony. The first volume *Die Wasserfälle von Slunj*, appeared in 1963, the second volume, *Der Grenzwald*, was to be his last uncompleted work and was published posthumously in 1967. He died of intestinal cancer on 23 December 1966.

Bibliography

Works published during lifetime (in German)

- *Gassen und Landschaft* (poems) (1923) ("Streets and Landscape")
- *Die Bresche* (novel) (1924) ("The Breach")
- *Das Geheimnis des Reichs* (novel) (1930) ("The Secret of the Realm")
- *Der Fall Gütersloh* (monograph on the painter Gütersloh) (1930)
- *Ein Mord, den jeder begeht* (novel) (1938) ("A Murder, That Everyone Commits")
- *Ein Umweg* (novel) (1940) ("A Detour")
- *Die erleuchteten Fenster oder die Menschwerdung des Amtsrates Julius Zihal* (novel) (1951) ("The Lighted Window")
- *Die Strudlhofstiege oder Melzer und die Tiefe der Jahre* (novel) (1951) ("The Strudelhof Steps")
- *Das letzte Abenteuer* (novella) (1953) ("The Last Adventure")

o *Die Dämonen. Nach der Chronik des Sektionsrates Geyrenhoff* (novel) (1956) ("The Demons")
o *Ein Weg im Dunkeln* (poems) (1957) ("A Way Into the Darkness")
o *Die Posaunen von Jericho* (novella) (1958) ("The Trombones of Jericho")
o *Grundlagen und Funktion des Romans* (essay) (1959) ("Principles and function of the Novel")
o *Die Peinigung der Lederbeutelchen* (short stories) (1959) ("The Torment of the Leather Bag")
o *Die Merowinger oder die totale Familie* (novel) (1962) ("The Merovingians or The Total Family")
o *Roman Nr.7/I. Die Wasserfälle von Slunj* (novel) (1962) ("Novel No. 7/I. The Waterfalls of Slunj")
o *Tangenten. Tagebuch eines Schriftstellers 1940 1950* (diaries) (1964)
o *Unter schwarzen Sternen* (short stories) (1966)
o *Meine neunzehn Lebensläufe und neun andere Geschichten* (short stories) (1966)

Published posthumously

o *Roman No. 7/II. Der Grenzwald* (novel) (1967) ("Novel No. 7/II. The Border Forest")
o *Frühe Prosa. Die Bresche Jutta Bamberger - Das Geheimnis des Reichs* (early prose) (1968)
o *Repertorium* (an ABC of ideas & concepts) (1969)
o *Die Wiederkehr der Drachen* (essays) (1970) ("The Return of the Dragons")
o *Die Erzählungen* (collected short stories) (1972)
o *Commentarii 1951 bis 1956. Tagebücher aus dem Nachlaß* (diaries) (1976)
o *Commentarii 1957 bis 1966. Tagebücher aus dem Nachlaß* (diaries) (1986)
o *Heimito von Doderer / Albert Paris Gütersloh: Briefwechsel 1928 1962* (letters) (1986)
o *Die sibirische Klarheit* (early texts from years in Russia) (1991)
o *Gedanken über eine zu schreibende Geschichte der Stadt Wien* (essay, facsimile of author's handwriting) (1996) ("Thoughts About a Not Yet Written History of the City of Vienna")
o *Tagebücher 1920 1939* (diaries) (1996)
o *Von Figur zu Figur* (letters to Ivar Ivask) (1996)
o *Seraphica. Montefal.* (2009: 2 posthumously published early stories)[1]

Websites (URLs online)

o Comprehensive page on the author
o www.doderer-gesellschaft.org - The Heimito von Doderer Society's website with information on the author, translations of his works into English etc.
o Heimito von Doderer fonds at University of Victoria, Special Collections

See also Wilhelm Carl von Doderer and Heinrich von Hügel

A hyperlinked version of this chapter is at http://booksllc.net?q=Heimito%5Fvon%5FDoderer

13

HELENE MIGERKA

Helene Migerka (September 13, 1867, Brno - March 26, 1928, Graz) was an Austrian poetess, novelist, was a daughter of the Austrian feminist and writer Katharina Kämpffat (1844, Tilsit - 1922)[1] and Franz Migerka (1828, Reintal - 1915, Vienna)[2].

Literary works

- *Gedichte*, 1889
- *Neue Gedichte*, 1895
- *Das Glück der Häßlichen und andere Skizzen und Satiren*, 1913
- *Der neue Besen*, 1920

References (URLs online)

- http://www.onb.ac.at/ariadne/vfb/bio_migerkahelene.htm
- http://www.aeiou.at/aeiou.encyclop.m/m618471.htm;internal&action=
  _setlanguage.action?LANGUAGE=en

- 1. http://www.onb.ac.at/ariadne/vfb/bio_migerkakath.htm
- 2. http://www.onb.ac.at/ariadne/vfb/bio_migerkafranz.htm

See also: Migerka

A hyperlinked version of this chapter is at http://booksllc.net?q=Helene%
5FMigerka

14

HERMYNIA ZUR MÜHLEN

---

[1]

Hermynia Zur Mühlen (1883-1951) was an Austrian writer and translator.

Works

- *Schupomann Karl Müller* (1924)
- *Unsere Töchter, doe Nazinnen* Our Daughters, the Nazis (1935)
- *We Poor Shadows* (1943)
- *Came the Stranger* (1946)

Sources

- *Bloomsbury Guide to Women's Literature*

L. Gossman, "The Red Countess: Four Stories," *Common Knowledge.*, vol. 15 (2009), 59-91. Ailsa Wallace, *Hermynia Zur Muhlen: The Guises of Socialist*

Fiction (Oxford University Press, 2009) Manfred Altner, *Hermynia Zur Muhlen; Eine Biographie,* (Bern: Peter Lang, 1997)

A hyperlinked version of this chapter is at http://booksllc.net?q=Hermynia%5FZur%5FM%C3%BChlen

15

HERTHA PAULI

Hertha Pauli (* 4. September 1906 in Vienna; 9. February 1973 in Long Island, New York) was as journalist, author and actress.

Biography

Hertha Ernestine Pauli was the daughter of the feminist Bertha Schütz and the medical scientist Wolfgang Pauli. Her brother was the Nobel Prize winner Wolfgang Pauli. From 1927 to 1933 she played different small roles at the Max Reinhardt Theatre in Berlin and was allied with Ödön von Horváth. From 1933 to 1938 she lived in Vienna, edited the "Österreichische Korrespondenz" and published biographical novels, for example about the feminist Bertha von Suttner.[1]

After the Anschluss she emigrated to France. In Paris she belonged to the circle of Joseph Roth, knew the American journalist Eric Sevareid, and wrote for *Resistance*. In 1940, after the Nazis occupied France, she fled with the writer Walter Mehring through Marseilles, the Pyrenees and Lisbon. With the aid of Varian Fry and the Emergency Rescue Committee, she made her way to the United States.[2]

After her arrival in America she described her flight in the journal Aufbau.[3] In the following years she wrote books about Alfred Nobel and the Statue of Liberty. Her books for children, in particular, had some success. These books included "Silent Night. The Story of a Song" (1943), in which she explained the origin of the carol. She married Ernst Basch (pen name E.B. Ashton), with whom she had collaborated on "I Lift My Lamp." Her last book was autobiographical and described the time after the Nazi's union with France.[4]

Works

- Toni. Ein Frauenleben für Ferdinand Raimund, 1936
- Nur eine Frau. Bertha von Suttner, 1937
- Alfred Nobel, Dynamite King, Architect of Peace, 1942
- Silent Night. The Story of a Song", 1943
- Story of the Christmas Tree, 1944
- St. Nicholas Travels, 1946
- I Lift my Lamp, The Way of a Symbol, 1948
- The Golden Door, 1949
- Three Is a Family, 1955
- Bernadette and the Lady, 1956
- Her Name Was Sojourner Truth
- The Secret of Sarajevo: The Story of Franz Ferdinand and Sophie, 1966
- Break of Time, 1972

References (URLs online)

- 1. http://www.univie.ac.at/biografiA/PauliTagung/BerichtHerthaPauli-Tagung.htm
- 2. Varian Fry: Surrender on Demand. Random House, 1945
- 3. Three parts, published on 11.10.40, 25.10.40 and 01.11.40. http://deposit.d-nb.de/online/exil/exil.htm
- 4. Pauli, Hertha: Break of Time. Hawthorn Book, 1972.

Literature

- *Between Sorrow and Strength: Women Refugees of the Nazi Period*, edited by Sibylle Quack, David Lazar, Christof Mauch. Cambridge University Press, 2002.
- Marino, Andy, *American Pimpernel: The Man who Saved the Artists on Hitler's Death List*. Hutchinson, 1999.
- Pfanner, Helmut F., *Exile in New York: German and Austrian Writers After 1933*. Wayne State University Press, 1983.
- Stern, Guy, 'Hertha Pauli'. In: Stern, Guy, *Literatur im Exil*, Bd.2. Ismaning 1989.

Websites (URLs online)

- "Eine Brücke über den Riss der Zeit...". Das Leben und Wirken der Journalistin und Schriftstellerin Hertha Pauli

o The German and Jewish intellectual émigré collection of the university at Albany: http://images.google.com/imgres?imgurl=http://library.albany.edu/speccoll/images/emigremtg.jpg&imgrefurl=http://library.albany.edu/speccoll/emigre.htm&h=1015&w=1401&sz=224&hl=en&start=16&um=1&usg=__Dj6mdAhhm-vnJPt55dn8XjUZwOU=&tbnid=roYmvRrs-r5paM:&tbnh=109&tbnw=150&prev=/images%3Fq%3D%2522hertha%2Bpauli%2522%26um%3D1%26hl%3Den%26lr%3D

o Works by or about Hertha Pauli in libraries (WorldCat catalog)

A hyperlinked version of this chapter is at http://booksllc.net?q=Hertha%5FPauli

16

HUGO VON HOFMANNSTHAL

Hugo Laurenz August Hofmann von Hofmannsthal (February 1, 1874 July 15, 1929), was an Austrian novelist, librettist, poet, dramatist, narrator, and essayist.

Life

Hofmannsthal was born in Landstraße, Vienna, the son of an upper-class Austrian mother, Anna Maria Josefa Fohleutner (18521904), and an AustrianItalian bank manager, Hugo August Peter Hofmann, Edler von Hofmannsthal (18411915). His great-grandfather, Isaak Löw Hofmann, Edler von Hofmannsthal, from whom his family inherited the noble title "Edler von Hofmannsthal," was a Jewish merchant ennobled by the Austrian emperor. He began to write poems and plays from an early age. He met the German poet Stefan George at the age of seventeen and had several poems published in George's journal, *Blätter für die Kunst*. He studied law and later philology in Vienna but decided to devote himself to writing upon graduating in 1901. Along with Peter Altenberg and Arthur Schnitzler, he was a member of the avant garde group Young Vienna (*Jung Wien*).

In 1900, Hofmannsthal met the composer Richard Strauss for the first time. He later wrote libretti for several of his operas, including *Elektra* (1909), *Der Rosenkavalier* (1911), *Ariadne auf Naxos* (1912, rev. 1916), *Die Frau ohne Schatten* (1919), *Die ägyptische Helena* (1927), and *Arabella* (1933).

In 1901, he married Gertrud (Gerty) Schlesinger, the daughter of a Viennese banker. Gerty, who was Jewish, converted to Christianity before their marriage. They settled in Rodaun, not far from Vienna, and had three children.

In 1912 he adapted the 15th century English morality play *Everyman* as *Jedermann*, and Jean Sibelius (amongst others) wrote incidental music for it. The play later became a staple at the Salzburg Festival.

During the First World War Hofmannsthal held a government post. He wrote speeches and articles supporting the war effort, and emphasizing the cultural tradition of AustriaHungary. The end of the war spelled the end of the old monarchy in Austria; this was a blow from which the patriotic and conservative-minded Hofmannsthal never fully recovered.

Nevertheless the years after the war were very productive ones for Hofmannsthal; he continued with his earlier literary projects, almost without a break. In 1920, Hofmannsthal, along with Max Reinhardt, founded the Salzburg Festival. His later plays revealed a growing interest in religious, particularly Roman Catholic, themes. Among his writings was a screenplay for a film version of *Der Rosenkavalier* (1925) directed by Robert Wiene.

On July 13, 1929, his son Franz committed suicide. Two days later, Hofmannsthal himself died of a stroke at Rodaun (now part of Liesing). He was buried wearing the habit of a Franciscan tertiary, as he had requested.

Thought

On October 18, 1902, Hofmannsthal published a fictive letter in the Berlin Daily, *Der Tag* (*The Day*) titled simply "Ein Brief" ("A Letter"). It was purportedly written in 1603 by Philip, Lord Chandos to Francis Bacon. In this letter Chandos says that he has stopped writing because he has "lost completely the ability to think or to speak of anything coherently"; he has given up on the possibility of language to describe the world. This letter reflects the growing distrust of and dissatisfaction with language that so characterizes the Modern era, and Chandos's dissolving personality is not only individual but societal.

Growing up the son of a wealthy merchant who was well connected with the major artists of the time, Hofmannsthal was raised in what Carl Schorske refers to as "the temple of art". This perfect setting for aesthetic isolation allowed Hofmannsthal the unique perspective of the privileged artist, but also allowed him to see that art had become a flattened documenting of humanity, which took our instincts and desires and framed them for viewing without acquiring any of the living, passionate elements. Because of this realization, Hofmannsthals idea of the role of the artist began to take shape as someone who created works that would inspire or inflame the instinct, rather than merely preserving it in a creative form. He also began to think that the artist should not be someone isolated and left to his art, but rather a man of the world, immersed in both politics and art.

Hofmannsthal saw in English culture the ideal setting for the artist. This was because the English simultaneously admired Admiral Nelson and John Milton, both war heroes and poets, while still maintaining a solid national identity. "In [Hofmannsthals] view, the division between artist (writer) and man of action (politician, explorer, soldier) does not exist in England. Britain provides her subjects with a common base of energy which functions as equilibrium, a force lacking in fragmented Germany" (Weiss). This singular and yet pragmatic identity must have appealed to Hofmannsthal to a certain degree due to the large scale fragmentation of Austria at the time, which was in the throes of radical nationalism and anti-Semitism, a nation in which the progressive artist and the progressive politician were growing more different and hostile to each other by the day.

Present-day descendants

Rodolphe von Hofmannsthal, great-grandson of Hugo, is married to Lady Frances von Hofmannsthal, née Armstrong-Jones, daughter of the 1st Earl of Snowdon (former husband of Princess Margaret, Countess of Snowdon) and his second wife, Lucy Mary Davies.

Selected works

Plays

- *Der Tor und der Tod* (1891)
- *Der Tod des Tizian* (1901)
- *Elektra* (1904)
- *Ödipus und die Sphinx* (1906)
- *Die Frau im Fenster* (1909)
- *Jedermann* (1911)
- *Der Schwierige* (1921)
- *Das Salzburger grosse Welttheater* (1922)
- *Der Turm* (1925)

Libretti

- *Elektra* (1909)
- *Der Rosenkavalier* (1911)
- *Ariadne auf Naxos* (1912, rev. 1916)

- *Die Frau ohne Schatten* (1919)
- *Die ägyptische Helena* (1927)
- *Arabella* (1933)

References (URLs online)

- This article incorporates material from the German Wikipedia article.
- Broch, Hermann (Author), Steinberg, Michael P. (Translator). *Hugo von Hofmannsthal and His Time: The European Imagination, 1860-1920*, University Of Chicago Press, 1984, ISBN 978-0226075167.
- McClatchy, J. D. (editor). *The Whole Difference: Selected Writings of Hugo von Hofmannsthal*, Princeton University Press, 2008, ISBN 978-0691129099. Chapter 1 contains a brief biography.
- Schorske, Carl E. *Fin-de-Siècle Vienna: Politics and Culture*, 1980
- Weiss, Winifred. *Comparative Literature*. Vol 25, no. 1. (Winter, 1973) pp. 6067

Websites (URLs online)

- Hugo von Hofmannthal Resource Center
- University of Washington Vienna 1900 Page

A hyperlinked version of this chapter is at http://booksllc.net?q=Hugo%5Fvon% 5FHofmannsthal

17

JAKOV LIND

Jakov Lind (born *Heinz Landwirth*, February 10, 1927 in Vienna February 16, 2007 in London) was an Austrian-British writer. As an 11-year old boy from a Jewish family, he left Austria after the Anschluss, found temporary refuge in Holland, and succeeded in surviving inside Nazi Germany by assuming a Dutch identity. After a literary apprenticeship in Israel, he moved to London, where he wrote, in German, the short stories and novels on which his stature as a major European writer is based: *Soul of Wood*, *Landscape in Concrete*, and *Ergo*. Lind began writing in English and the stories in *The Stove* were the first written in his new language. His stories have been translated into English, German, Danish, Swedish, Dutch, French, Italian, Norwegian, Finnish, Spanish, Hungarian, and Czech. His work been adapted into plays, operas, and films. A book about his life has also been published,*Writing After Hitler: the Work of Jakov Lind* (2001).

Books

- o   o *Soul of Wood* (1964)
    - o Landscape in Concrete (1966)

- *Ergo: A Comedy* (1967)
- *Counting My Steps* (1969)
- *Numbers: A Further Autobiography* (1972)
- *The Trip to Jerusalem* (1973)
- *The Silver Foxes Are Dead and Other Plays* (1968)
- *Travels to the Enu: The Story of a Shipwreck* (1982)
- *The Stove* (1983)
- *The Inventor* (1987)
- *Crossing: the Discovery of Two Islands* (1991)

Websites (URLs online)

- Jakov Lind web site
- *Journey Through the Night - a short film adapted from Lind's story, by Joram ten Brink*
- *The Guardian* obituary
- Jakov Lind at Open Letter Books
- Jakov Lind at New York Review Books Classics
- Jakov Lind at The Quarterly Conversation

See also: Lind and Landwirth

A hyperlinked version of this chapter is at http://booksllc.net?q=Jakov%5FLind

18

JOHN WRAY (NOVELIST)

John Henderson (1971-), better known by his pen name **John Wray**, is a novelist and regular contributor to The New York Times Magazine. Born in Washington, DC of an American father and Austrian mother, he is a citizen of both countries. He grew up in Buffalo, New York, attended the prestigious Nichols School for his high school education, and currently lives in Brooklyn.

Wray's first novel, *The Right Hand of Sleep*, was published in 2001 and received a Whiting Writers' Award. In connection with his second novel, *Canaans Tongue*, he did a 600-mile tour by raft on the Mississippi River in 2005. In 2007 Wray was chosen by Granta magazine as one of the "Best of Young American Novelists." His third novel, *Lowboy*, was published on March 3, 2009.

Wray was also frontman of Brooklyn band Marmalade, who released the album *Beautiful Soup*[1] in 2003. As part of the promotional activities surrounding the release of Lowboy, he recorded subway musicians for a Lowboy MP3 soundtrack.

Websites (URLs online)

- ○ [2] What Can 'Lowboy' Author John Wray Do With Literary Success? – New York Magazine, March 1, 2009
- ○ An Author Indulges His Inner Twain by David Carr in the July 5, 2005 New York Times
- ○ Wray interviewed about Lowboy on NPR's Book Tour by Lynn Neary
- ○ John Wray Official Website
- ○ 2009 podcast interview at The Bat Segundo Show
- ○ A review of John Wray's Lowboy

A hyperlinked version of this chapter is at http://booksllc.net?q=John%5FWray%5F%28novelist%29

19

JOSEPH DELMONT

Joseph Delmont, born **Karl Pick**, or Josef Pollack (8 May 1873 12 March 1935) was an Austrian film director of some 200 films, largely shorts, in which he was noted for his innovative use of beasts of prey. He was also a cameraman, actor and screenplay writer. During later life he was active as an author.

Life

Delmont was born as Karl Pick in Lichtenau im Waldviertel, Austria, and grew up as a performer, latterly a trapeze artist, in a travelling circus. After a training as a metal worker, he re-joined the circus as an animal trainer and lion tamer, in which capacity he travelled the world. During 1901 he visited the United States, and stayed there in order to work as director of an animal business.

After visiting several shows of the new medium of film and becoming interested in it, Delmont started to make his own films during 1903 for the film production company Vitagraph. These were short Westerns, one-act movies or one-reelers lasting only few minutes. During 1905 he made his first two-act movie.

During 1910 he returned to Vienna where among other things he worked for the Österreichisch-Ungarische Kinoindustrie (later Wiener-Kunstfilm) as a cameraman, and was thus cameraman, and also technical director and director of scenery, on the oldest Austrian drama film to survive entire: *Der Müller und sein Kind* of 1911. Soon afterwards however he went to Germany. In Berlin, in among other places the Rex-Ateliers, he directed, sometimes together with Harry Piel as co-director, and Fred Sauer, Curt Bois and Ilse Bois as actors, a series of adventurous, action-packed, dramatic fantasy films. The sensational part of these films was the, for the time, extraordinary film footage of beasts of prey, for which his films were well-known.

For making his movies Delmont travelled in Panama, Portugal, England, France, Spain and the Netherlands.

During 1925 he ended his film career: his last film project was to direct *Der Millionenraub im Rivieraexpreß* that year. Instead he devoted himself principally to authorship, with which he had dabbled since 1892. By the time of his death during 1935 he had written several novels and short stories, and many newspaper articles. Besides detective stories and non-fiction work about his experiences with animals, he also wrote adventure and crime novels. With *"Der Ritt auf dem Funken"* (1928) he published a futuristic science fiction novel about the possibility in the near future of travelling with vehicles on electric currents.

Delmont died during 1935 in Bad Pystian, now Pieany, Slovakia.

Filmography

The following is a selected list of films, both short and long, directed by Delmont. In many he also wrote the screenplay or appeared as an actor.

- *Der Müller und sein Kind* (I), 1910 (Germany; screenplay only)
- *Der Müller und sein Kind* (II), 1911 (Austria; camera and technical direction)
- *Der Streikbrecher*, 1911 (Germany)
- *Mutter und Sohn*, 1911 (Germany)
- *Verirrte Seelen*, 1911 (Germany)
- *Das sechste Gebot*, 1912 (Germany)
- *Der Fremde*, 1912 (Germany)
- *Die Puppe*, 1912 (Germany)
- *Schuld und Sühne*, 1912 (Germany; screenplay)
- *Der wilde Jäger*, 1912 (Germany; screenplay)
- *Dichterlos*, 1912 (Germany)
- *Das Sterben im Walde*, 1912 (Germany; screenplay, actor)
- *Das Recht aufs Dasein*, 1913 (Germany; crime film; actor with, among others, Ilse Bois; 880 metres)
- *Der letzte Akkord*, 1913 (Germany; screenplay)
- *Das rote Pulver*, 1913 (Germany; screenplay)

- *Das Tagebuch eines Toten*, 1913 (Germany)
- *Auf einsamer Insel*, 1913 (Germany; screenplay, actor)
- *Der geheimnisvolle Klub*, 1913 (Germany; actor with, among others, Ilse Bois, Fred Sauer; 851 metres)
- *Der Desperado von Panama*, 1914 (Germany; actor)
- *Ein Erbe wird gesucht*, 1915 (Germany)
- *Ein ungeschriebenes Blatt*, 1915 (Germany; screenplay)
- *Der Silbertunnel*, 1915 (Germany)
- *Titanenkampf*, 1916 (Germany; screenplay)
- *Theophrastus Paracelsus*, 1916 (Germany; screenplay)
- *Die Töchter des Eichmeisters*, 1916 (Germany; screenplay)
- *Das Geheimnis des Waldes*, 1917 (Austria 1917; co-director with Hans Otto Löwenstein, screenplay)
- *Der Bastard*, 1919 (Germany; screenplay)
- *Margot de Plaisance*, 1919 (Germany; screenplay)
- *Der Kampf der Geschlechter*, 1919 (Germany; screenplay)
- *Die Geächteten*, 1919 (Germany; screenplay)
- *Die Insel der Gezeichneten*, 1920 (Germany)
- *Madame Recamier / Des Großen Talma letzte Liebe*, 1920 (Germany)
- *Der König der Manege*, 1921 (Germany; co-author of screenplay, Schauspiel)
- *Die eiserne Faust*, 1921 (Germany)
- *Julot, der Apache*, 1921 (Germany; screenplay)
- *Der Mann aus Stahl*, 1922 (Germany)
- *Der Sieg des Maharadscha*, 1923 (Germany)
- *Marco unter Gauklern und Bestien*, 1923 (Germany)
- *Mater Dolorosa*, 1924 (Germany)
- *Um eine Million*, 1924 (Germany; co-director, screenplay)
- *Der Millionenraub im Rivieraexpreß*, 1925-27 (Germany/France 1925-1927)

Literary works

The German National Library knows of 15 novels and 11 other works by Joseph Delmont, of which the following are a selection:

- *Wilde Tiere im Film: Erlebnisse aus meinen Filmaufnahmen in aller Welt.* Dieck, Stuttgart 1925 (non-fictional account of his experiences with animals; went through 14 editions)
- *Die Stadt unter dem Meere.* Leipzig 1925 (novel)
- *In Ketten.* Fr. Wilh. Grunow, Leipzig 1926 (reprinted several times in the following years under the title *Juden in Ketten*)
- *Von lustigen Tieren und dummen Menschen: Eine Melange.* Neue Berliner Verlags-GmbH, Berlin 1927
- *Abenteuer mit wilden Tieren: Erlebnisse e. Raubtierfängers* Enßlin & Laiblin, Reutlingen 1927 (part of the collection "Aus weiter Welt")
- *Der Gefangene der Wüste* Neufeld & Henius, Berlin 1927
- *Die Sieben Häuser: Wanderfahrten e. Lausbuben.* Grethlein & Co., Leipzig 1927
- *Der Ritt auf dem Funken: Phantastischer Zukunftsroman.* O. Janke, Berlin 1928

- ○ *Der Casanova von Bautzen.* Leipzig 1931; new edition Lusatia-Verlag, Bautzen 2005
- ○ *Die Abenteuer des Johnny Kilburn.* F. W. Grunow, Leipzig 1934

References (URLs online)

- ○ Winkler, Gerhard, 2005: *Joseph Delmont: 1873 - 1935; Abenteurer - Filmer - Schriftsteller; sein Leben - seine Filme - seine Bücher.* St. Pölten: Dokumentationsstelle für Literatur in Niederösterreich Literaturedaktion Niederösterreich

Sources / Websites (URLs online)

- ○ Joseph Delmont in the German National Library catalogue (German)
- ○ Joseph Delmont at the Internet Movie Database

A hyperlinked version of this chapter is at http://booksllc.net?q=Joseph%5FDelmont

---

20

JOSEPH ROTH

Joseph Roth (September 2, 1894 in Brody - May 27, 1939 in Paris) was an Austrian novelist, best known for his family saga *Radetzky March* (1932), and for his novel of Jewish life, *Job* (1930).

Habsburg empire

Roth grew up in Brody, a small town near Lviv in East-Galicia, part of the easternmost reaches of the Austro-Hungarian empire. Jewish culture played an important role in the life of the town.

After high school, Joseph Roth moved to Lviv to begin his university studies in 1913. Only one year later, he settled in Vienna to study philosophy and German literature at the local university. In 1916, Roth quit his university course and volunteered to serve in the Imperial Habsburg army fighting the First World War. This experience had a major and long-lasting influence on his life. So, too, did the collapse of the Habsburg Empire in 1918, which marked the beginning of a pronounced sense of 'homelessness' that was to feature regularly in his work.

Germany

In 1920 he moved to Berlin, where he worked as a highly successful journalist for the *Neue Berliner Zeitung*, then from 1921 for the *Berliner Börsen-Courier*. Later he became a features correspondent for the well-known liberal *Frankfurter Zeitung*, travelling widely throughout Europe. In 1925 he spent an influential period working in France and never again resided permanently in Berlin. In the late 1920s, his wife Friederike had become schizophrenic, which threw Roth into a deep crisis both emotionally and financially.

In 1923 Roth's first (unfinished) novel, *The Spider's Web*, was serialized in an Austrian newspaper and he achieved moderate success as a writer throughout the 1920s with a series of novels documenting life in post-War Europe. Only upon publication of *Job* and *Radetzky March* did he achieve real acclaim as a novelist.

From 1930, Roth's fiction became less concerned with contemporary society, with which he had become increasingly disillusioned, and during this period his work frequently evoked a melancholic nostalgia for life in imperial Central Europe prior to 1914. He often portrayed the fate of homeless wanderers looking for a place to live, in particular Jews and former citizens of the old Austria-Hungary, who, with the downfall of the monarchy, had lost their only possible *Heimat* or true home.

In his later works in particular, Roth appeared to wish that the monarchy could be restored in all its old glamour, even though at the start of his career he had written under the codename of "Red Joseph". His longing for a more tolerant past may be partly explained as a reaction against the nationalism of the time which finally culminated in National Socialism.

The novel *The Radetzky March* (1932) and the story *Die Büste des Kaisers* (*The Bust of the Emperor*) (1935) are typical of this late phase. In the novel *The Emperor's Tomb* Roth describes the fate, up until Germany's annexation of Austria in 1938, of a cousin of the hero of *The Radetzky March*. Of his works which deal with Judaism, the novel *Job* is the best-known.

Paris

Online image: The grave of Joseph Roth at the Thiais cemetery

On January 30, 1933, the day Adolf Hitler became Reich Chancellor, Roth, a prominent liberal Jewish journalist, left Germany. He would spend most of the next decade in Paris, a city he loved.

Shortly after Hitler's rise to power, in February 1933, Roth wrote in a prophetic letter to his friend, Austrian writer Stefan Zweig:

"You will have realized by now that we are drifting towards great catastrophes. Apart from the private - our literary and financial existence is destroyed - it all leads to a new war. I won't bet a penny on our lives. They have succeeded in establishing a reign of barbarity. Do not fool yourself. Hell reigns."[1]

From 1936 to 1938, he had a romantic relationship with Irmgard Keun. They worked together, traveling to various cities such as Paris, Wilna, Lemberg, Warsaw, Vienna, Salzburg, Brussels and Amsterdam.

Without intending to deny his Jewish origins, Roth considered his relationship to Catholicism very important, and in the final years of his life, he may even have converted; translator Michael Hofmann states in the preface to the collection of essays *Report from a Parisian Paradise* that Roth "was said to have had two funerals, one Jewish, one Catholic."

Despite suffering from chronic alcoholism, Roth remained prolific until his premature death in Paris in 1939. His final novella, *The Legend of the Holy Drinker* (1939), is amongst his finest, and chronicles the attempts made by an alcoholic vagrant to regain his dignity and honour a debt.

Joseph Roth is interred in the Thiais cemetery to the south of Paris.

Works

- *Das Spinnennetz* (The Spider's Web) (1923)
- *Hotel Savoy* (Hotel Savoy) (1924)
- *Die Rebellion* (The Rebellion) (1924)
- *April. Die Geschichte einer Liebe* (April: The History of a Love) (1925)
- *Der blinde Spiegel* (The Blind Mirror) (1925)
- *Juden auf Wanderschaft* (The Wandering Jews) (1927)
- *Die Flucht ohne Ende* (The Flight without End) (1927)
- *Zipper und sein Vater* (Zipper and His Father) (1928)
- *Rechts und links* (Right and Left) (1929)
- *Der stumme Prophet* (The Silent Prophet) (1929)
- *Hiob* (Job (novel)) (1930)
- *Radetzkymarsch* (The Radetzky March) (1932)
- *Der Antichrist* (The Antichrist) (1934)
- *Tarabas* (1934)
- *Beichte eines Mörders* (Confession of a Murderer) (1936)
- *Das falsche Gewicht* (Weights and Measures) (1937)
- *Die Kapuzinergruft* (The Emperor's Tomb) (1938)
- *Die Legende vom heiligen Trinker* (The Legend of the Holy Drinker) (1939)
- *Die Geschichte von der 1002. Nacht* (The String of Pearls) (1939)
- *Der Leviathan* (The Leviathan) (1940)

References (URLs online)

○ 1. 38. Hell reigns. - From a letter of Joseph Roth to Stefan Zweig, February 1933, page 70, Hitlers Machtergreifung - dtv dokumente, Edited by Josef & Ruth Becker, Deutscher Taschenbuch-Verlag, Second edition, Munich, Germany 1992, ISBN 3-423-02938-2

Bibliography

○ Martin Mauthner: *German Writers in French Exile, 1933-1940*, Vallentine Mitchell, London, 2007(ISBN 978 0 85303 540 4).

See also (online edition)

○ Exilliteratur

Websites (URLs online)

○ JRO - Joseph Roth Online

A hyperlinked version of this chapter is at http://booksllc.net?q=Joseph%5FRoth

21

JOSEPH VON SONNENFELS

Joseph von Sonnenfels (1732, Nikolsburg/Mikulov, Moravia April 25, 1817, Vienna) was an Austrian and German jurist and novelist

He is a son of **Perlin Lipmann** (1705 - 1768), and brother of Franz Anton von Sonnenfels. Joseph, who was baptized in his early youth, received his elementary education at the gymnasium of his native town Nikolsburg, and then studied philosophy at the University of Vienna. In 1749, he joined the regiment "Deutschmeister" as a private, advancing to the rank of corporal. On his discharge in 1754, he took a course in law at the University of Vienna, then he established himself as a counselor at law in the Austrian capital. From 1761 to 1763, he officiated as secretary of the Austrian "Arcierengarde". In 1763, he was appointed professor of political science at the University of Vienna, twice acting as rector magnificus. In 1779, he received the title of "Wirklicher Hofrath", and was in 1810 elected president of the Academy of Sciences, a position which he held until his death.

From 1765 to 1767 and from 1769 to 1775 Sonnenfels was editor of "Der Mann ohne Vorurtheil", in which paper he defended the liberal tendencies in literature.

He improved the Vienna stage especially through his critical work "Briefe über die Wienerische Schaubühne", in which he attacked the harlequin of the Vienna theater, causing this figure to be eliminated from the personnel of the stage.

He was chiefly instrumental in bringing about the abolition of torture in Austria (1776). Sonnenfels' attitude toward Lessing placed the former in a very unfavorable light, as it was due to his intrigues and jealousy that Lessing was not called to Vienna. Sonnenfels was severely condemned for his action in this affair.

He is also the dedicatee of Ludwig van Beethoven's Piano Sonata No. 15, Op. 28, which was published in 1801.

Sonnenfels was among the leaders of the Illuminati movement in Austria, and a friend and patron of Mozart.

Literary works

Among Sonnenfels' many works may be mentioned:

- *"Specimen Juris Germanici de Remediis Juris, Juri Romano Incognitis,"* Vienna, 1757;
- *"Ankündigung einer Teutschen Gesellschaft in Wien,"* ib. 1761;
- *"Betrachtungen über die Neuen Politischen Handlungsgrundsätze der Engländer,"* ib. 1764;
- *"Grundsätze der Polizei, Handlung und Finanzwissenschaft,"* ib. 176567 (8th ed. 1819);
- *"Briefe über die Wienerische Schaubühne,"* ib. 1768 (reedited by Sauer, ib. 1884);
- *"Von der Verwandlung der Domänen in Bauerngüter,"* ib. 1773;
- *"Ueber die Abschaffung der Tortur,"* Zurich, 1775 (2d ed. Nuremberg, 1782);
- *"Abhandlung über die Aufhebung der Wuchergesetze,"* Vienna, 1791;
- *"Handbuch der Innern Staatsverwaltung,"* ib. 1798
- *"Ueber die Stimmenmehrheit bei Criminalurtheilen,"* Vienna, 1801 (2d ed. 1808)

His *"Gesammelte Werke"* appeared in 10 volumes (Vienna, 178387), and contained most of his belletristic works, poems, and dramas.

References (URLs online)

- *This article incorporates text from the 19011906 Jewish Encyclopedia article "Sonnenfels" by Isidore Singer and Frederick T. Haneman, a publication now in the public domain.*
- *The Masonic Thread of Mozart by Katherine Thomson (page 16). Published in London 1977.*

A hyperlinked version of this chapter is at http://booksllc.net?q=Joseph%5Fvon%5FSonnenfels

22

LEO PERUTZ

Leopold Perutz (November 2, 1882, Prague - August 25, 1957, Bad Ischl) was an Austrian novelist and mathematician. He was born in Prague and was thus a citizen of the Austro-Hungarian Empire. He lived in Vienna until the Nazi *Anschluss* in 1938, when he emigrated to Palestine.

According to the biographical note on the Arcade Publishing editions of the English translations of his novels, Leo was a mathematician who formulated an algebraic equation which is named after him; he worked as a statistician for an insurance company. He was related to the biologist Max Perutz.[1]

During the 1950s he returned occasionally to Austria, spending the summer and autumn months in the market town of St. Wolfgang in the Salzkammergut resort region and in Vienna. He died in the Austrian spa town of Bad Ischl in 1957. He wrote his first novel, *The Third Bullet*, in 1915 while recovering from a wound sustained in the First World War. In all Perutz wrote eleven novels, which gained the admiration of Jorge Luis Borges, Italo Calvino, Ian Fleming, Karl Edward

Wagner and Graham Greene. Wagner cited Perutz' novel *The Master of the Day of Judgement* as one of the thirteen best non-supernatural horror novels.[2]

Overview

Perutz' novels are short and are usually historical novels combining fast-paced adventure with a metaphysical twist. Austrian fellow novelist Friedrich Torberg once characterized Perutz' literary style as the possible result of a little infidelity of Franz Kafka and Agatha Christie. *By Night Under the Stone Bridge* is an episodic work whose separate stories are bound together by the illicit love shared, in their dreams, by a Jewish woman and the Emperor Rudolf II. In the posthumously-published *Leonardo's Judas*, da Vinci's quest for an appropriate face to give the betrayer in his *Last Supper* is interwoven with the squabble between an usurer and the merchant to whom he owes money. The title of *Saint Peter's Snow*, which is set in what was then the present day (1932), refers to a drug which induces religious fervour; the Nazis, understandably, did not care for it. *The Master of the Day of Judgement* is a decidedly different mystery story about the circumstances surrounding an actor's death in the early twentieth century, and *Little Apple* concerns a First World War soldier's obsessive quest for revenge.

Novels by Perutz in English translation

(Dates of publication are for the original German-language editions)

- *From Nine to Nine* (1918)
- *The Marquis of Bolibar* (1920)
- *The Master of the Day of Judgement* (1921)
- *Turlupin* (1924)
- *Little Apple* (1928)
- *Saint Peter's Snow* (1933)
- *The Swedish Cavalier* (1936)
- *By Night under the Stone Bridge* (1952)
- *Leonardo's Judas* (1959)

References (URLs online)

- 1. Max Ferdinand Perutz OM FRS, obituary by Alan R. Fersht.
- 2. N. G. Christakos, "Three By Thirteen: The Karl Edward Wagner Lists" in *Black Prometheus: A Critical Study of Karl Edward Wagner*, ed. Benjamin Szumskyj, Gothic Press 2007.

Read On

- Hans Harald Müller: *Leo Perutz* (biography, München: Verlag C. H. Beck, 1992)
- Neuhaus, Dietrich: *Errinerung und Schrecken. DieEinheit von Geschichte, Phantastik und Mathematik im Werk Leo Perutz* (Frankfurt am Main: P. Lang, 1984)

- o Brigitte Forster, Hans Harald Müller (Hrsg.): *Leo Perutz. Unruhige Träume - Abgründige Konstruktionen. Dimensionen des Werks, Stationen der Wirkung.* (Wien: Sonderzahl, 2002) ISBN 3-85449-197-2.
- o Ulrike Siebauer: *Leo Perutz Ich kenne alles. Alles, nur nicht mich.* (biography, Gerlingen: Bleicher, 2000)

Websites (URLs online)

- o Brief biography in German
- o Appreciation by Jessica Amanda Salmonson
- o German and international bibliography

A hyperlinked version of this chapter is at http://booksllc.net?q=Leo%5FPerutz

23

LILIAN FASCHINGER

Lilian Faschinger (born April 29, 1950) is an Austrian novelist, short story writer, poet, and literary translator.

Born in Tschöran, Carinthia, Faschinger read English and History at the University of Graz. She won international recognition with her novel, *Magdalena Sünderin* (1995), which was translated into 17 languages.

Lilian Faschinger lives in Vienna.

Novels

- *Die neue Scheherazade* (1986)
- *Lustspiel* (1989)
- *Magdalena Sünderin* (1995) (*Magdalena the Sinner*, translated by Shaun Whiteside)
- *Wiener Passion* (1999)
- *Stadt der Verlierer* (2007)

Her translations into German include works by Paul Bowles, Janet Frame, Elizabeth Smart, and Gertrude Stein.

A hyperlinked version of this chapter is at http://booksllc.net?q=Lilian%5FFaschinger

24

LUDWIG ANZENGRUBER

Ludwig Anzengruber (November 29, 1839 December 10, 1889) was an Austrian dramatist, novelist and poet. He was born and died in Vienna.

Origins

The Anzengruber line originated in the district of Ried im Innkreis in Upper Austria. Ludwig's grandfather, Jakob Anzengruber, was a farm-worker on the Obermayr estate at Weng near Hofkirchen an der Trattnach. His father, Johann Anzengruber, left the family home at an early age and moved to Vienna, where he found work as a bookkeeper in the treasury of the Austrian crown lands. In 1838 he married Maria Herbich, the daughter of a petit bourgeois pharamacist. It is not surprising that the social standing of his parents - his father, from peasant stock, and his mother, a petty bourgeois - regularly played an important role in Ludwig Anzengruber's later works.

Ludwig's greatest influence in becoming a dramatist was his father who himself had been a secret poet in the style of Friedrich Schiller, but without success. Only one of his plays, on the subject of Berthold Schwarz, was produced, and probably only because of the spectacular explosion at the end; his other works gathered dust in the drawer of his desk.

Early life and career

Ludwig was only 5 years old when his father died in 1844. His mother, who was to become the most important person in his life as the years went on, tried to make ends meet with her meager widow's pension of 166 guilders and 40 kreuzers. In 1854 when Ludwigs grandmother, who had been supporting her daughter and grandchild substantially, died, his home and living arrangements became even worse. Financial emergencies drained their savings, but Ludwig's mother was ready to make any sacrifice (including taking up work as a seamstress) so that he could study at the Paulaner elementary school from 1847 to 1850 and then at the Piarist high school from 1851 to 1853. In 1855 he dropped out of school due to increasingly bad grades and from 1856 to 1858 he was an apprentice at the Sallmeyer bookstore. During his employment at the bookstore he was able to read a great deal, but after disagreements with his master his apprenticeship came to an abrupt end.

At the age of 19, after a severe bout of typhoid, Ludwig decided to become an actor. Over the next ten years he tried his luck as a professional actor, travelling with different acting troupes throughout the provinces of Austria. He worked as a supporting actor in many a second-rate theatre, without, however, displaying any marked talent, and he never made the breakthrough to success, although his stage experience later stood him in good stead. One thing that hindered him was the dialect that he spoke, a dialect he was never able completely to get rid of. From 1866 he returned to live in Vienna again. During this time he wrote several dramas and some short stories, but these were unsuccessful.

Creative period

In 1869 he found his way back into bourgeois society, when he took a job as a clerk (probably because he badly needed money) in the imperial police headquarters in Vienna. In 1870 under the pseudonym "L. Gruber" he wrote what was to be his breakthrough, his anti-clerical drama *Der Pfarrer von Kirchfeld* (*The Priest from Kirchfeld*). The play was first produced at the *Theater an der Wien*, and its premiere on November 5 was a great success. Heinrich Laube, the head of the *Burgtheater*, wrote an enthusiastic review and through this Ludwig struck up a friendship with Peter Rosegger. His overnight success meant that the *police official (4th class)* could step off the career ladder of the civil service and devote himself entirely to literature, which saved him from conflict between being a poet and his duty to his office.

In 1873, despite his mother's warnings, Anzengruber married the 16-year-old Adelinde Lipka (1857-1914). His young bride, the sister of his childhood friend Franz Lipka, was not up to the demands of practical life, and thus there were repeated crises in their marriage, although Ludwig's considerable debts and very close relationship with his mother were often also to blame for this. Despite their three children, divorce was inevitable, and in 1889 the couple separated officially.

The following years were very successful for Anzengruber. His plays were produced throughout Europe, though his mother was never able to fully share in his success, as she had died in 1875. From April 1882 until May 1885 he was the editor of the Viennese paper *Die Heimat* (*The Homeland*), in May 1884 he became a contributing editor of *Le Figaro* and in August 1888 he became the editor of the *Wiener Bote* (*Vienna Messenger*).

In September 1888 he was given the position of dramaturg for the *Volkstheater Wien* in Vienna, which opened on September 14, 1889 with his piece *Der Fleck auf der Ehr* (*The Stain on Honour*).

At the end of November, the dramatist, who was only fifty years old, became sick with anthrax, and not two weeks later died as a result of blood poisoning.

Selected works

Dramas

Anzengruber's plays are mostly of Austrian peasant life, and although somewhat melancholy in tone are interspersed with bright and witty scenes.

- *Der Pfarrer von Kirchfeld* (*The Priest from Kirchfeld*) (folk play with music in 4 acts) - Premiere: Theater an der Wien 5. November 1870
- *Der Meineidbauer* (*The Perjuring Farmer*) (folk play with music in 3 acts) - Premiere: Theater an der Wien 9 December 1871
- *Die Kreuzelschreiber* (peasant comedy with music in 3 acts) - Premiere: Theater an der Wien 12 October 1872
- *Elfriede* (play in 3 acts) - UA: Carl-Theater 24. April 1873
- *Die Tochter des Wucherers* (*The Usurer's Daughter*) (Play with music in 5 acts) - Premiere: Theater an der Wien 17 October 1873
- *Der G'wissenswurm* (*The Worm of Conscience*) (peasant comedy with music in 3 acts) - Premiere: Theater an der Wien 19. September 1874
- *Hand und Herz* (*Hand and Heart*) (tragedy in 4 acts) - Premiere: Wiener Stadttheater 31 December 1874
- *Doppelselbstmord* (*Double Suicide*) (tragedy in 3 acts) - Premiere: Theater an der Wien 1 February 1876
- *Der ledige Hof* (play in 4 Acts) - UA: Theater an der Wien 27 January 1877
- *Das vierte Gebot* (*The Fourth Commandment*) (play in 4 acts) - Premiere: Josefstädter Theater 29 December 1878

Novels

○ *Der Schandfleck* (*The Mark of Shame*) - 1st edition: 1877; 2nd edition: 1884
○ *Der Sternsteinhof* (*The Sternstein Manor*) - 1885

Anzengruber also published various short stories and tales of village life collected under the title *Wolken und Sunn'schein* (1888).

References (URLs online)

This article is a translation of the corresponding German Wikipedia article which lists the following reference works: -

○ Ludwig Anzengruber, *Ausgewählte Werke. Eine Einführung in das Leben and das Werk des Dichters* Erwin Heinzel. Vienna: Kremayr & Scheriau 1966.
○ Franz Baumer, *Ludwig Anzengruber*; Weilheim (Stöppel) 1989.
○ Anton Bettelheim, *Ludwig Anzengruber*; Berlin 1891.
○ Anton Büchner, *Zu Ludwig Anzengrubers Dramentechnik*; Dissertation, Gießen 1911.
○ Elisabeth Hanke, *Ludwig Anzengrubers Kalendergeschichten*; Dissertation, Wien 1950.
○ Alfred Kleinberg, *Ludwig Anzengruber. Ein Lebensbild.* Stuttgart: Cotta, 1921.
○ Aloys Klocke, *Die religiöse and weltanschaulich-ethische Problematik bei Ludwig Anzengruber*; Dissertation, Freiburg i. Br. 1955.
○ Louis Koessler; *Ludwig Anzengruber - auteur dramatique*; Dissertation, Straßburg 1943.
○ Werner Martin, *Der Kämpfer. Atheismus bei Anzengruber*; Berlin 1960.
○ Edward McInnes, *Ludwig Anzengruber and the popular dramatic tradition*; in: Maske and Kothurn 21 (1975), 135-152.
○ Peter Rosegger, *Peter Rosegger - Ludwig Anzengruber. Briefwechsel: 1871 1889.* Konstanze Fliedl; Karl Wagner (Editors). Vienna: Böhlau, 1995. (Literatur in der Geschichte, Geschichte in der Literatur ; 33)
○ Emma Spröhnle, *Die Psychologie der Bauern bei Anzengruber*; Dissertation, Tübingen 1930.

Anzengruber's collected works, with a biography, were published in 10 vols. in 1890 (3rd ed. 1897); his correspondence has been edited by A. Bettelheim (1902). See:

○ L. Rosner, *Erinnerungen an L. Anzengruber* (1890)
○ H. Sittenberger, *Studien zur Dramaturgie der Gegenwart* (1899)
○ S. Friedmann, *L. Anzengruber* (1902).

Websites (URLs online)

○ Works by Ludwig Anzengruber at Project Gutenberg
○ (German) Texts from Ludwig Anzengruber at Projekt Gutenberg-DE

○ (German) Short biography in German

This article incorporates information from the German Wikipedia.

See also: Anzengruber

A hyperlinked version of this chapter is at http://booksllc.net?q=Ludwig%5FAnzengruber

25

REUBEN ASHER BRAUDES

Reuben As(c)her Braudes, *Reuven Asher Braudes* (Hebrew: ; Russian: ; 1851, Wilna - October 18, 1902, Vienna) was a Lithuania-born Hebrew novelist and journalist.

Educated on the usual Talmudic lines of Jewish education, he came early under the influence of the Maskilim.

In 1868 Braudes became a contributor to "*Ha-Lebanon*" (Hebrew:), a Hebrew weekly published by Brill in Mainz, and for several years he devoted his pen to topics of the day and to criticism.

It was as a novelist, however, that he was to make a mark in Hebrew literature. In 1874 he published in "*The Dawn*" (Hebrew:), a monthly edited by Smolenskin at Vienna, his first story, entitled "*The Mysteries of the Zephaniah Family*" (Hebrew:), a tale of great promise from its style and vivid descriptions. The next year appeared his second novel, "*The Repentant*" (Hebrew:), which was followed by one entitled "*Religion and Life*"; Hebrew:), treating of Jewish life. This remarkable work was published in "*The Morning Light*" (Hebrew:), issued by Gottlober at Lemberg in 1875.

Another novel of great merit, "*The Two Extremes*" (Hebrew:), appeared in Lemberg in 1885. In this book Braudes pictures in vivid colors the Orthodox and Reformed camps in modern Israel.

In 1882, at the time of the anti-Semitic riots in Russia, Braudes plunged into the Zionist movement and became one of its foremost advocates. To foster this idea he went to Romania, and began the publication at Bucharest of "*Yehudit*", a weekly in Yiddish. At the end of two years, however, Braudes was expelled from the country.

In 1891 he went to Cracow, Galicia, and started a weekly in Hebrew, "*The Time*" (Hebrew:). This paper existed for nine months, when, for lack of funds, its publication was suspended. Nothing of importance from Braudes' pen appeared in recent years.

References (URLs online)

  o *This article incorporates text from the 1901 1906 Jewish Encyclopedia, a publication now in the public domain.* ([1])

By Louis Ginzberg & Max Raisin

A hyperlinked version of this chapter is at http://booksllc.net?q=Reuben%5FAsher%5FBraudes

26

ROBERT HAMERLING

Robert Hamerling (March 24, 1830 July 13, 1889) was an Austrian poet.

Biography

Hamerling was born into a poor family at Kirchberg am Walde in Lower Austria. He displayed an early genius for poetry; his youthful attempts at drama excited the interest and admiration of some influential persons. Owing to their assistance young Hamerling was able to attend the gymnasium in Vienna and afterwards the University of Vienna.

In 1848 he joined the students' legion, which played a large part in the revolutions of the capital, and in 1849 shared in the defence of Vienna against the imperialist troops of Alfred I, Prince of Windisch-Grätz. After the collapse of the revolutionary movement he was obliged to hide for a couple of weeks to escape arrest.

For the next few years he pursued his studies in natural science and philosophy, and in 1855 became master at the Gymnasium at Trieste. For many years he was ill, and in 1866 retired on a pension, which in acknowledgment of his literary works was increased by the government to a sum sufficient to enable him to live carefree until he died at his villa in Stiftingstal near Graz, Austria.

A popular edition of Hamerlings works in four volumes was published by M. M. Rabenlechner (Hamburg, 1900).

Evaluations

1911 Encyclopædia Britannica

The 1911 Encyclopædia Britannica characterizes Hamerling as one of the most remarkable poets of the modern Austrian school, describing his imagination as rich and his poems as full of life and colour. What it terms his most popular poem, *Ahasver in Rom* (1866), of which the emperor Nero is the central figure, is said to show at its best what is alleged to be the author's brilliant talent for description. Among his other works, 1911 Britannica mentions *Venus im Exil* (1858); *Der König von Sion* (1869), characterized as a generally recognized masterpiece; *Die sieben Todsünden* (1872) *Blätter im Winde* (1887); *Homunculus* (1888); *Amor und Psyche* (1882).

The 1911 Britannica goes on to describe his novel, *Aspasia* (1876), as giving a finely-drawn description of the Periclean age, but like his tragedy *Danton und Robespierre* (1870), somewhat stilted, which it thought showed that Hamerling's genius, though rich in imagination, was ill-suited for the realistic presentation of character.

References (URLs online)

- "Hamerling, Robert". *Encyclopædia Britannica* (11th ed.). 1911. This work in turn cites:
  - Robert Hamerling, *Stationen meiner Lebenspilgerschaft* (Stations of my life pilgrimage, autobiography, 1889)
  - Robert Hamerling, *Lehrjahre der Liebe* (Years of learning from love, autobiography, 1890)
  - M. M. Rabenlechner, *Hamerling, sein Leben und seine Werke*, i. (Hamburg, 1896)
  - M. M. Rabenlechner, a short biography of Robert Hamerling (Dresden, 1901)
  - R. H. Kleinert, *R. Hamerling, ein Dichter der Schönheit (R. Hamerling a poet of beauty, Hamburg, 1889)*
  - Aurelius Polzer, *Hamerling, sein Wesen und Wirken* (Hamerling, his essence and legacy, Hamburg, 1890).

Websites (URLs online)

- Robert Hamerling in the German National Library catalogue (German)

- ○ Robert-Hamerling-Museum
- ○ Thomas Meyer: Hamerling and Steiner antisemitic?
- ○ Robert Hamerling In: Roman History Project. Datenbank. University of Innsbruck.

A hyperlinked version of this chapter is at http://booksllc.net?q=Robert%
5FHamerling

27

ROBERT MUSIL

Robert Mathias *Edler von*[1] **Musil** (November 6, 1880 - April 15, 1942) was an Austrian writer. His unfinished long novel *The Man Without Qualities* (German: *Der Mann ohne Eigenschaften*) is generally considered to be one of the most important modernist novels.

Biography

Online image: Plate in Brno

Musil was the son of **Alfred** *Edler von*[1] **Musil** (1846, Temesvár - 1924) and his wife **Hermine Bergauer** (1853, Linz - 1924), who lived together with an unrelated "uncle" **Heinrich Reiter** (born 1856), the houseguest in the Musil family. The elder Musil was an engineer, firstly family moved to Chomutov til October 1881, and appointed in 1891 to the chair of Mechanical Engineering at the German Technical University in Brno, and awarded a hereditary peerage in the Austro-Hungarian empire shortly before it collapsed. He was a second cousin of Alois Musil, the famous orientalist[2]

Hermine Bergauer was a daughter of a Bohemian German engineer **Franz (Xaver von) Bergauer** (December 3, 1805, Horschowitz - October 11, 1886, Linz)[3]

The younger Musil had a short stature, but was strong and skilled at wrestling, and by his early teens already more than his parents could handle. Accordingly they sent him to military boarding school at Eisenstadt (1892-1894) and then Hranice, in that time also known as *Mährisch Weißkirchen*, (1894-1897). These school experiences are reflected in his first novel, *Die Verwirrungen des Zöglings Törless* (*The Confusions of Young Törless*).

After graduating as a cadet, Musil briefly studied at a military college in Vienna during the fall of 1897, but then switched to engineering, joining his father's department at Brno. During his college career he studied engineering by day, but at night read literature and philosophy, and went to the theater and art exhibits. Nietzsche, Dostoyevsky, Ralph Waldo Emerson, and Ernst Mach were particular interests of his college years. Musil finished his studies in three years, then in 1902-1903 served as an unpaid assistant to Professor Julius Carl von Bach, in Stuttgart. During this time he began work on *Young Törless*.

Even then, however, Musil was growing tired with engineering and the limited worldview of engineers, and rather than settle into an engineering career, he launched a new round of doctoral studies (1903-1908) in psychology and philosophy at the University of Berlin under the renowned Professor Carl Stumpf. In 1905, Musil had met Martha Marcovaldi (née Heinemann, January 21, 1874 - November 6, 1949) who was in subsequent years to become his wife. She had already been widowed and remarried, with two children, and was seven years older than Musil. In the midst of these studies his first novel, Young Törless, was published in 1906.

In 1909, Musil completed his doctorate and was offered a position by Professor Alexius Meinong, at the University of Graz, which he turned down to concentrate on literature. Over the next two years, he wrote and published two stories ("The Temptation of Quiet Veronica" and "The Perfecting of a Love") collected in *Vereinigungen* (*Unions*) published in 1911. During this same year, Martha's divorce was completed and Musil married her. Until this time, Musil had been supported by his family, but he now found employment first as a librarian in the Technical University of Vienna, and then in an editorial role with the *Berlin Literary Journal*, during which time he worked on a play entitled *Die Schwärmer* (*The Enthusiasts*), which was eventually published in 1921.

When World War I began, Musil joined the Army, stationed first in Tirol, and then away from danger at Austria's Supreme Army Command in Bolzano. In 1916 Musil visited Prague and met Franz Kafka whose work he held in high esteem, as he did the work of Bohemian poet Rainer Maria Rilke. At the "Memorial Service for Rilke in Berlin", Musil remarked that Rilke was "undervalued" for most of his life, and by the time of his death, he had "turned into 'a delicate, well-matured liqueur suitable for grown-up ladies'",[4] but that his work is "too demanding" to be "considered relaxing".[5] After the war's end, and the collapse of the Austro-Hungarian empire, Musil returned to his literary career in Vienna. He published a collection of short stories, *Drei Frauen* (*Three Women*), in 1924, and then in 1930 and 1932 the first two volumes of his masterpiece, *Der Mann ohne Eigenschaften* (*The Man Without Qualities*). The novel deals with the moral and intellectual decline of the Austro-Hungarian Empire through the eyes of the book's protagonist Ulrich, an ex-mathematician who has failed to engage with the world around him in a manner that would allow him to possess 'qualities'. It is set in Vienna on the eve of World War I.

The Man Without Qualities brought Musil only mediocre commercial success. Though he was nominated for the Nobel Prize, he felt he did not receive the recognition he deserved. He sometimes expressed annoyance at the success of more famous colleagues like Thomas Mann (or Hermann Broch) who admired his work deeply, and moved by his material poverty, tried to shield him against quotidian worries and encouraged him to further his literary work, even though Musil was initially critical of Mann.

In the early 1920s Musil lived mostly in Berlin. In Vienna Musil was a frequent visitor of Eugenie Schwarzwald's salon (the model of Diotima in *The Man Without Qualities*). In 1932 The Robert Musil Society was founded in Berlin on the initiative of Thomas Mann. The same year Thomas Mann was asked to name an eminent contemporary novel and he cited exclusively *The Man Without Qualities*. In 1936 Musil had his first stroke.

The last years of Musil's life were dominated by Nazism and World War II; the Nazis banned his books. He saw early Nazism first-hand while living in Berlin from 1931-1933. In 1938, when Austria became a part of the Third Reich, Musil and his Jewish wife Martha left for exile in Switzerland, where he died on April 15, 1942. Martha wrote *Franz Theodor Csokor* [6] that taking off his clothes in the bathroom, maybe when doing gymnastics or just making an hefty movement, he had been hit by a stroke and, when she found him a few minutes later, did not look dead at all but so alive with some mockery and astonishment on his face. He was 61. Only eight people were present at his cremation. Martha cast his ashes into the woods of Mont Salève.[7] From the galleys Musil had retrieved from the printer and been reworking until his very last day she published part 3 of *The Man Without Qualities* in 1943 and died in Rome in 1949 .

After his death Musil's work was almost forgotten in German speaking countries. His writings began to reappear during the early 1950s. The first translation of *The Man Without Qualities* in English was published by Ernst Kaiser and Eithne Wilkins in 1953, 1954 and 1960. An improved translation by Sophie Wilkins and Burton Pike, containing extensive selections from unpublished drafts in the two-volume American edition, appeared in 1995.

Timeline

1880 November 6 Robert Musil born in Klagenfurt. Father Engineer Alfred Musil, mother Hermine.

1881-1882 The Musils move to Komotau, Bohemia.

1882-1891 The Musils move to Steyr (Oberöstereich). Robert attends the *Volksschule* and the first grade of the *Realgymnasium*.

1891-1892 Moves to Brunn. Attends the *Realschule*.

1892-1894 Attends the *Militär-Unterrealschule* in Eisenstadt.

1894-1897 Attends the *Militär-Oberrealschule* in Mährisch-Weisskirchen (the present-day Hranice in the Czech Republic) During his working with artileries Musil discovers his interest in technique.

1897 Attends the *Technische Militärakademie* in Vienna.

1898-1901 Quits officer training and starts studies at the Technical University of Brunn. His father had been a professor there since 1890. First literary attempt, and first diary notations.

1901 PhD exams.

1901-1920

1901-1902 Musil enlists in the infantry regiment of Freiherr von Hess Nr. 49 in Brunn

1902-1903 Moves to Stuttgart to work at the University. Works on his first novel *Die Verwirrungen des Zöglings Törless*

1903-1908 Takes up a philosophy study; his majors are "logic and experimental psychology".

1905 In his diaries he makes the first notes that will eventually lead to *Der Mann ohne Eigenschaften*.

1906 *Die Verwirrungen des Zöglings Torless* is published. Developed an apparatus to research colour experience in people.

1908 *Beiträge zur Beurteilung der Lehren Machs* is the title of his doctoral thesis with which he promotes in philosophy, natural science and mathematics. Declines an offer to upgrade his last military rank to an equal civilian rank in favour of writing.

1908-1910 Works in Berlin as an editor for the magazine *Pan* and on his *Vereinigungen* and *Die Schwärmer*.

1911-1914 Librarian at the Technical University of Vienna.

1911 On April 15 Musil marries Martha Marcovaldi. *Vereinigungen* is published.

1912-1914 Editor for several literary magazines, including *Die Neue Rundschau*.

1914-1918 During World War I, Musil is officer at the Italian front. Decorated several times.

1916-1917 July-April: publishes the "Soldaten-Zeitung".

1917 On October 22 Alfred Musil ennobled. This nobility is hereditary: thus, Musil will be belong to the nobility to his death (Robert Edler von Musil).

1918 Takes up writing again.

1919-1920 Works for the Information Service of the Austrian foreign department in Vienna.

1920 April-June: lives in Berlin. Meets Ernest Rowohlt who will become, in 1923, his publisher and will remain so.

1920-1922 Adviser for army matters in Vienna.

1921-1931 Works as theater critic, essayist and writer in Vienna. Works on *Der Mann ohne Eigenschaften*.

1921 The play *Die Schwärmer* is published.

1923-1929 Is vice-president of *Schutzverbandes deutscher Schriftsteller in Östereich*. Meets Hugo von Hofmannsthal, who is president of the foundation.

1923 Awarded the Kleist Prize for *Die Schwärmer*. On December 4 *Vinzenz und die Freundin bedeutender Männer* is premiered in Berlin.

1924 On January 24 his mother and on October 1 his father die. Awarded the art prize of the city of Vienna. *Drei Frauen* is published.

1927 Holds a speech on the occasion on the death of Rainer Maria Rilke in Berlin.

1929 April 4 premiere of *Die Schwärmer*. In spite of protests by Musil, the play is shortened and therefore incomprehensible, according to Musil. In the autumn awarded the Gerhart Hauptmann award.

1930 The first two parts of *Der Mann ohne Eigenschaften* are published. In spite of critical support, the financial situation is precarious.

1931-1933 Lives and works in Berlin.

1932 Foundation of a *Musil-Gesellschaft* by Kurt Glaser in Berlin. The foundation aims to provide Musil with the means necessary to continue working on his novel. At the end of the year the third part of *Der Mann ohne Eigenschaften* is published.

1933 In May Musil leaves Berlin, with his wife Martha. Via Karlsbad and Schloss Pottenstein (Potstejn) they eventually reach Vienna.

1934-1938 After the dismantling of the Berlin *Musil-Gesellschaft*, a new one is founded in Vienna.

1935 Lecture for the Internationalen Schriftstellerkongress für die Verteidigung der Kultur" in Paris.

1936 Publishes his collection of thoughts, observations and stories *Nachlass zu Lebzeiten*. Suffers a stroke.

1938 Via Northern Italy Musil and his wife flee to Zürich. Two days after their arrival, on September 4, they are having tea at Thomas Mann's home in Küsnacht.

1939 In July moves to Geneva. Musil continues to work on his novel under the worst financial circumstances, and grows lonelier with exile. Thanks to the Zürich vicar Robert Lejeune, Musil receives some financial support, including from the American couple Henry Hall and Barbara Church. In Germany and Austria *Der Mann ohne Eigenschaften* and *Nachlaß zu Lebzeiten* are banned and this ban is extended to all of his works in 1941.

1942 April 15 Musil dies in Geneva.

1943 Martha Musil publishes the unfinished remains of *Der Mann ohne Eigenschaften* on her own account.

1952-1957 Adolf Frisé publishes the complete works of Robert Musil at Rowohlt.

Bibliography

- *Die Verwirrungen des Zöglings Törleß* (*The Confusions of Young Torless*, 1906), later made into a movie *Der junge Törless*
- *Vereinigungen* (1911) (*Unions* - a collection of two short stories)
- *Die Schwärmer* (1921)
- *Vinzenz und die Freundin bedeutender Männer* (1924)
- *Drei Frauen* (1924) (*Three Women* - a collection of three short stories)
- *Nachlaß zu Lebzeiten* (1936) (*Posthumous Papers of a Living Author* - a collection of short prose pieces)
- *Über die Dummheit* (1937)
- *Der Mann ohne Eigenschaften* (*The Man Without Qualities*, 1930, 1933, 1943, published in two volumes)

Further reading

- B. Pike, *Robert Musil: An Introduction to His Work*, Kennikat Press, 1961, reissued 1972, ISBN 0-8046-1546-2.

Websites (URLs online)

- Comprehensive site in Dutch and English
- The website of the Robert Musil Literature Museum
- Ted Gioia, "A Fresh Look at *The Man Without Qualities*," Great Books Guide

References (URLs online)

- 1. (since October 22, 1917)
- 2. [1]
- 3. Sammlung Bergauer (pdf), http://www.landesarchiv-ooe.at/xchg/SID-3DCFCFBE-EC088F9E/hs.xsl/1225_DEU_HTML.htm, http://zs.thulb.uni-jena.de/receive/jportal_jparticle_00011907
- 4. http://entertainment.timesonline.co.uk/tol/arts_and_entertainment/the_tls/article6836668.ece
- 5. Robert Musil, *Precision and Soul: Essays and Addresses*, trans. Burton Pike and David S. Luft (Chicago: U of Chicago P, 1995).
- 6. Der Monat 026/1950, pp. 185-189, on www.ceeol.com
- 7. Markus Kreuzwieser http://www.sbg.ac.at/exil/lecture_5023.pdf

See also: Musil and Bergauer

A hyperlinked version of this chapter is at http://booksllc.net?q=Robert%5FMusil

28

STEFAN ZWEIG

Stefan Zweig (November 28, 1881, Schottenring 14[1], Innere Stadt, Vienna, Austria February 22, 1942, Petrópolis, Brazil) was an Austrian novelist, playwright, journalist and biographer.

Life

Zweig was the son of Moritz Zweig (1845-1926), a wealthy Jewish textile manufacturer, and Ida Zweig née Brettauer (1854-1938), from a Jewish banking family. Joseph Brettauer did business for twenty years in Ancona, Italy, where his second daughter Ida was born and grew up, too. Zweig studied philosophy at the university of Vienna and in 1904 earned a doctoral degree with a thesis on "The Philosophy of Hippolyte Taine". Religion did not play a central role in his education. "My mother and father were Jewish only through accident of birth," Zweig said later in an interview. Yet he did not renounce his Jewish faith and wrote repeatedly on Jewish themes. Although his essays were published in the *Neue Freie Presse*, whose literary editor was the Zionist leader Theodor Herzl, Zweig was not attracted to Herzl's Jewish nationalism.

In the First World War Zweig served in the Archives of the Ministry of War, and soon acquired a pacifist stand like his friend Romain Rolland, winner of the Nobel Prize for Literature 1915. Zweig remained pacifist all his life and advocated the unification of Europe. Like Rolland, he wrote many biographies. His *Erasmus of Rotterdam* he called a "concealed self-portrayal" in *The World of Yesterday*.

Zweig fled Austria in 1934, following Hitler's rise to power in Germany. He then lived in England (in London and from 1939 in Bath) before moving to the United States in 1940. In 1941 he went to Brazil, where in 1942 he and his second wife Lotte (*née* Charlotte Elisabeth Altmann) committed suicide together in Petrópolis,[2] despairing at the future of Europe and its culture. "I think it better to conclude in good time and in erect bearing a life in which intellectual labour meant the purest joy and personal freedom the highest good on Earth," he wrote. His autobiography *The World of Yesterday* is a paean to the European culture he considered lost.

Work

Stefan Zweig was a prominent writer in the 1920s and 1930s. Though he is still well-known in many European countries, his work has become less familiar in the anglophone world. Since the 1990s there has been an effort on the part of several publishers (notably Pushkin Press and New York Review of Books) to get Zweig back into print in English.

Zweig is best known for his novellas (notably *The Royal Game, Amok*), novels (*Beware of Pity, Confusion of Feelings*, and the posthumously published *The Post Office Girl*) and biographies (notably *Erasmus of Rotterdam, Conqueror of the Seas: The Story of Magellan*, and *Mary, Queen of Scotland and the Isles*). At one time his works were published in English under the pseudonym 'Stephen Branch' (a translation of his real name) when anti-German sentiment was running high. His biography of Queen Marie-Antoinette was later adapted for a Hollywood movie, starring the actress Norma Shearer in the title role.

Zweig also provided the libretto for the 1934 opera *Die schweigsame Frau* (*The Silent Woman*) by Richard Strauss. Strauss famously defended him from the Nazi regime, by refusing to remove Zweig's name from the posters for the work's première in Dresden. As a result, Hitler refused to attend as planned, and the opera was banned after three performances. Zweig later would collaborate with Joseph Gregor, to provide Strauss with the libretto for one other opera, *Daphne*, in 1937. At least[3] one other work by Zweig received a musical setting: the pianist and composer Henry Jolles, who like Zweig had fled to Brazil to escape the Nazis, composed a song, "Último poema de Stefan Zweig",[4] based on "Letztes Gedicht", which Zweig wrote on the occasion of his 60th birthday in November 1941.[5]

There are important Zweig collections at the British Library and at the State University of New York at Fredonia. The British Library's Zweig Music Collection was donated to the library by his heirs in May 1986. It specialises in autograph music manuscripts, including works by Bach, Haydn, Wagner, and Mahler. It has been described as "one of the world's greatest collections of autograph manuscripts".[6] One particularly precious item is Mozart's "Verzeichnüß aller meiner Werke"[7] - that is, the composer's own handwritten thematic catalogue of his works.

Bibliography

The dates mentioned below are the dates of first publication in German.

Note: This bibliography is still incomplete. Please refer to the German version for more information.

Fiction

- *The Love of Erika Ewald*, 1904 (Original title: *Die Liebe der Erika Ewald*)
- *Burning Secret*, 1913 (Original title: *Brennendes Geheimnis*)
- *Letter from an Unknown Woman*, 1922 (Original title: *Brief einer Unbekannten*) - novella
- *Amok*, 1922 (Original title: *Amok*) - novella, initially published with several others in *Amok. Novellen einer Leidenschaft*
- *Fear*, 1925 (Original title: *Angst. Novelle*)
- *The Eyes of My Brother, Forever*, 1925 (Original title: *Die Augen des ewigen Bruders*)
- *The Invisible Collection* see *Collected Stories* below , (Original title: *Die Unsichtbare Sammlung*, first published in book form in 'Insel-Almanach auf das Jahr 1927'[8])
- *The Refugee*, 1927 (Original title: *Der Flüchtling. Episode vom Genfer See*).
- *Confusion of Feelings* or *Confusion: The Private Papers of Privy Councillor R. Von D*, 1927 (Original title: *Verwirrung der Gefühle*) - novella initially published in the volume *Verwirrung der Gefühle: Drei Novellen*
- *Twenty-Four Hours in the Life of a Woman*, 1927 (Original title: *Vierundzwanzig Stunden aus dem Leben einer Frau*) - novella initially published in the volume *Verwirrung der Gefühle: Drei Novellen*
- *Short stories*, 1930 (Original title: *Kleine Chronik. Vier Erzählungen*) - includes *Buchmendel*
- *Collected Stories*, 1936 (Original title: *Gesammelte Erzählungen*) - two volumes of short stories:
  1. *The Chains* (Original title: *Die Kette*)
  2. *Kaleidoscope* (Original title: *Kaleidoskop*). Includes: *Casual Knowledge of a Craft, Leporella, Fear, Burning Secret, Summer Novella, The Governess, Buchmendel, The Refugee, The Invisible Collection, Fantastic Night* and *Moonbeam Alley*
- *Beware of Pity*, 1939 (Original title: *Ungeduld des Herzens*) novel
- *The Royal Game* or *Chess Story* (Original title: *Schachnovelle*; Buenos Aires, 1942) - novella written in 1938-41, published posthumously
- *Clarissa*, 1981 unfinished novel, published posthumously

o *The Post Office Girl*, 1982 (Original title: *Rausch der Verwandlung. Roman aus dem Nachlaß*; *The Intoxication of Metamorphosis*) - unfinished novel, published posthumously, and in 2008 for the first time in English.

Biographies and Historical Texts

o Béatrice Gonzalés-Vangell, Kaddish et Renaissance, La Shoah dans les romans viennois de Schindel, Menasse et Rabinovici, Septentrion, Valenciennes, 2005, 348 pages.
o *Emile Verhaeren, 1910*
o *Three Masters: Balzac, Dickens, Dostoeffsky*, 1920 (Original title: *Drei Meister. Balzac Dickens Dostojewski*)
o *Romain Rolland. The Man and His Works*, 1921 (Original title: *Romain Rolland. Der Mann und das Werk*)
o *Nietzsche*, 1925 (Originally published in the volume titled: *Der Kampf mit dem Dämon. Hölderlin Kleist Nietzsche*)
o *Decisive Moments in History*, 1927 (Original title: *Sternstunden der Menschheit*)
o *Adepts in Self-Portraiture: Casanova, Stendhal, Tolstoy*, 1928 (Original title: *Drei Dichter ihres Lebens. Casanova Stendhal Tolstoi*)
o *Joseph Fouché*, 1929 (Original title: Joseph Fouché. *Bildnis eines politischen Menschen*)
o *Mental Healers: Franz Mesmer, Mary Baker Eddy, Sigmund Freud*, 1932 (Original title: *Die Heilung durch den Geist. Mesmer, Mary Baker-Eddy, Freud*)
o *Marie Antoinette: The Portrait of an Average Woman*, 1932 (Original title: *Marie Antoinette. Bildnis eines mittleren Charakters*) ISBN 4-87187-855-4
o *Erasmus of Rotterdam*, 1934 (Original title: *Triumph und Tragik des Erasmus von Rotterdam*)
o *Mary, Queen of Scotland and the Isles* or *The Queen of Scots*, 1935 (Original title: *Maria Stuart*)
o *The Right to Heresy: Castellio against Calvin*, 1936 (Original title: *Castellio gegen Calvin oder Ein Gewissen gegen die Gewalt*)
o *Conqueror of the Seas: The Story of Magellan*, 1938 (Original title: *Magellan. Der Mann und seine Tat*) ISBN 4-87187-856-2
o *Amerigo*, 1944 (Original title: *Amerigo. Geschichte eines historischen Irrtums*) - written in 1942, published the day before he died
o *Balzac*, 1946 - written, as Richard Friedenthal describes in a postscript, by Zweig in the Brazilian summer capital of Petrópolis, without access to the files, notebooks, lists, tables, editions and monographs that Zweig accumulated for many years and that he took with him to Bath, but that he left behind when he went to America. Friedenthal wrote that *Balzac* "was to be his *magnum opus*, and he had been working at it for ten years. It was to be a summing up of his own experience as an author and of what life had taught him." Friedenthal claimed that "The book had been finished," though not every chapter was complete; he used a working copy of the manuscript Zweig left behind him to apply "the finishing touches," and Friedenthal rewrote the final chapters (*Balzac*, translated by William and Dorothy Rose [New York: Viking, 1946], pp. 399, 402).

Plays

- *Tersites*, 1907 (Original title: *Tersites*)
- *Das Haus am Meer*, 1912
- *Jeremiah*, 1917 (Original title: *Jeremias*)

Other

- *The World of Yesterday* (Original title: *Die Welt von Gestern*; Stockholm, 1942) - autobiography
- *Brazil, Land of the Future* (Original title: *Brasilien. Ein Land der Zukunft*; Bermann-Fischer, Stockholm 1941)

Books on Stefan Zweig

- Elizabeth Allday, *Stefan Zweig: A Critical Biography*, J. Philip O'Hara, Inc., Chicago, 1972
- Alberto Dines, *Morte no Paraíso, a Tragédia de Stefan Zweig*, Editora Nova Fronteira 1981, (rev. ed.) Editora Rocco 2004
- Alberto Dines, *Tod im Paradies. Die Tragödie des Stefan Zweig*, Edition Büchergilde, 2006
- Randolph J. Klawiter, *Stefan Zweig. An International Bibliography*, Ariadne Press, Riverside, 1991
- Donald A. Prater, *European of Yesterday: A Biography of Stefan Zweig*, Holes and Meier Publ., (rev. ed.) 2003
- Marion Sonnenfeld (editor), *The World of Yesterday's Humanist Today. Proceedings of the Stafan Zweig Symposium*, texts by Alberto Dines, Randolph J. Klawiter, Leo Spitzer and Harry Zohn, State University of New York Press, 1983
- Friderike Zweig, *Stefan Zweig*, Thomas Y. Crowell Company, 1946 (An account of his life by his first wife)

Notes

- 1. Prof.Dr. Klaus Lohrmann *"Jüdisches Wien. Kultur-Karte"* (2003), Mosse-Berlin Mitte gGmbH (Verlag Jüdische Presse)
- 2. The United Press (February 24, 1942). "STEFAN ZWEIG, WIFE END LIVES IN BRAZIL". The New York Times. Retrieved 10 April 2009.
- 3. http://www.recmusic.org/lieder/z/zweig/
- 4. Musica Reanimata of Berlin, Henry Jolles accessed Jan 25, 2009
- 5. Biographical sketch of Stefan Zweig at Casa Stefan Zweig accessed September 28, 2008
- 6. The Zweig Music Collection at the British Library
- 7. Mozart's "Verzeichnüß aller meiner Werke" at the British Library Online Gallery[1] accessed October 14th, 2009
- 8. http://openlibrary.org/b/OL6308795M/unsichtbare_sammlung.

See also (online edition)

- Casa Stefan Zweig

Websites (URLs online)

- ○ Zweig Music Collection at the British Library
- ○ Stefan Zweig Collection at the Daniel A. Reed Library, State University of New York at Fredonia, Fredonia, NY
- ○ Stefan Zweig Online Bibliography, a wiki hosted by Daniel A. Reed Library, State University of New York at Fredonia, Fredonia, NY
- ○ StefanZweig.org
- ○ StefanZweig.de
- ○ PushkinPress.com English editions of Stefan Zweig's novellas
- ○ 'Beware of Pity' - The New York Review of Books at www.nybooks.com A lengthy review of Beware of Pity June 2006
- ○ Stefan Zweig: The Secret Superstar, from Intelligent Life Magazine

Categories: Young Vienna I Jewish writers I Austrian writers I Austrian novelists I Austrian dramatists and playwrights I Austrian biographers I Austrian journalists I Austro-Hungarian writers I Austro-Hungarian Jews I Czech-Austrian Jews I Austrians of German descent I People from Innere Stadt I Jewish refugees I Austrian refugees I Austrian exiles I People who emigrated to escape Nazism I Austrian expatriates in Brazil I Writers who committed suicide I Drug-related suicides in Brazil I 1881 births I 1942 deaths

Views

- ○ Article
- ○ Discussion
- ○ Edit this page
- ○ History

Personal tools

- ○ Try Beta
- ○ Log in / create account

Navigation

- ○ Main page
- ○ Contents
- ○ Featured content
- ○ Current events
- ○ Random article

Search

Interaction

- ○ About Wikipedia

- o Community portal
- o Recent changes
- o Contact Wikipedia
- o Donate to Wikipedia
- o Help

Toolbox

- o What links here
- o Related changes
- o Upload file
- o Special pages
- o Permanent link
- o Cite this page

Print/export

- o Create a book
- o Download as PDF
- o Printable version

Languages

- o Brezhoneg
- o Català
- o esky
- o Dansk
- o Deutsch
- o Eesti
- o Español
- o Esperanto
- o Euskara
- o Français
- o Gaeilge
- o Hrvatski
- o Ido
- o Íslenska
- o Italiano
- o Kurdî
- o Latina
- o Lietuvi
- o Magyar
- o Nederlands
- o Norsk (bokmål)
- o Norsk (nynorsk)
- o Occitan
- o Polski
- o Português

- Român
- Shqip
- Simple English
- Slovenina
- Srpskohrvatski /
- Suomi
- Svenska
- Türkçe
- Ting Vit

- This page was last modified on 16 March 2010 at 14:39.
- Text is available under the Creative Commons Attribution-ShareAlike License;additional terms may apply.See Terms of Use for details.
Wikipediapsy"D2 is a registered trademark of the Wikimedia Foundation, Inc., a non-profit organization.
- Contact us
- Privacy policy
- About Wikipedia
- Disclaimers

A hyperlinked version of this chapter is at http://booksllc.net?q=Stefan%5FZweig

29

SUSANNA KUBELKA

Susanna Kubelka von Hermanitz is a German-speaking writer living in France.

She was born in September 1942 in Linz (Austria). Having left high school she briefly worked as primary school teacher before graduating in English literature. In 1977 she took a PhD with a thesis on The way women were represented in the 18th century English novel[1]. Later she worked as a journalist for the Vienna newspaper *Die Presse*. She lived and worked in Australia and in England for 4 years. She is divorced and since 1981 she has permanently settled down in Paris (France). She claims to favour a vegetarian life style.

Her first book *Over Forty at Last* was published in 1980. Her most successful novel is *Ophelia Learns to Swim* of 1987. Her most extensive novel *Das gesprengte Mieder* (*The Broken Girdle*; not translated yet) came out in 2000.

Her books have been translated in 29 languages and are published in Germany by Verlagsgruppe Lübbe, in France by Editions Belfond (none in print) and in the USA by MacMillan Publishing Company.

Susanna Kubelka is the sister of the Austrian experimental film maker Peter Kubelka.

Works

- *Endlich über vierzig. Der reifen Frau gehört die Welt* (1980)
- *Ich fang nochmal an. Glück und Erfolg in der zweiten Karriere* (1981)
- *Burg vorhanden, Prinz gesucht. Ein heiterer Roman* (1983)
- *Ophelia lernt schwimmen. Der Roman einer jungen Frau über vierzig* (1987)
- *Mein Wien* (1990)
- *Madame kommt heute später* (1993)
- *Das gesprengte Mieder* (2000)
- *Der zweite Frühling der Mimi Tulipan* (2005)

English translations:

- *Over Forty at Last: How to Ignore the "Middle Life" Crisis and Make the Most Out of the Best Years of Your Life*, Macmillan (1982) ISBN 0025671502

Bibliography

- *Kubelka, Susanna (1942-): An article from: Contemporary Authors*, Thomson Gale (2007)

Websites (URLs online)

- Susanna Kubelka Her entry in The Internet Movie Database

References (URLs online)

- 1. Susanna Kubelka, *The Eighteenth Century Novel Heroine - a changing ideal. A study of novel heroines from Aphra Behn to Jane Austen*, Wien 1977, Univ. Diss., 2. Februar 1977

A hyperlinked version of this chapter is at http://booksllc.net?q=Susanna% 5FKubelka

30

THOMAS BERNHARD

Thomas Bernhard (born **Nicolaas Thomas Bernhard**, February 9, 1931 February 12, 1989) was an Austrian playwright and novelist. He is widely considered to be one of the most important German-speaking authors of the postwar era.

Life

Thomas Bernhard was born in 1931 in Heerlen, Netherlands as an illegitimate child to **Herta Fabjan** (1904-1950) and the carpenter **Alois Zuckerstätter** (1905-1940).

Bernhard spent much of his early childhood with his maternal grandparents in Vienna and Seekirchen, near Salzburg. His mother's subsequent marriage in 1936 occasioned a move to Traunstein, Bavaria.

Bernhard's grandfather, the author Johannes Freumbichler (de), pushed for an artistic education for the boy, including musical instruction. Bernhard went to elementary school in Seekirchen and later attended various schools in Salzburg including the *Johanneum* which he left in 1947 to start an apprenticeship with a grocer.

Bernhard's *Lebensmensch* (companion for life), whom he cared for alone in her dying days, was Hedwig Stavianicek (1894 - 1984), a woman more than thirty-seven years his senior, whom he met in 1950, the year of his mother's death and one year after the death of his beloved grandfather. She was the major support in his life and greatly furthered his literary career. Thomas Bernhard's public persona was asexual.[1]

Online image: *Thomas Bernhard's House*, Video by Christiaan Tonnis, 2006

Suffering throughout his youth from an intractable lung disease (tuberculosis), Bernhard spent the years 1949 to 1951 at the sanatorium in Grafenhof. He trained as an actor at the Mozarteum in Salzburg (1955-1957) and was always profoundly interested in music: his lung condition, however, made a career as a singer impossible. After that he began work briefly as a journalist, then as a full-time writer.

Bernhard died in 1989 in Gmunden, Upper Austria. His attractive house in Ohlsdorf-Obernathal 2 where he had moved in 1965 is now a museum and centre for the study and performance of Bernhard's work. In his will, which aroused great controversy on publication, Bernhard prohibited any new stagings of his plays and publication of his unpublished work in Austria. His death was announced only after his funeral.

Work

Often criticized in Austria as a *Nestbeschmutzer* (one who dirties his own nest) for his critical views, Bernhard was highly acclaimed abroad.

His work is most influenced by the feeling of being abandoned (in his childhood and youth) and by his incurable illness, which caused him to see death as the ultimate essence of existence. His work typically features loners' monologues explaining, to a rather silent listener, his views on the state of the world, often with reference to a concrete situation. This is true for his plays as well as for his prose, where the monologues are then reported *second hand* by the listener.

His main protagonists, often scholars or, as he calls them, *Geistesmenschen*, denounce everything that matters to the Austrian in tirades against the "stupid populace" that are full of contumely. He also attacks the state (often called "Catholic-National-Socialist"), generally respected institutions such as Vienna's Burgtheater, and much-loved artists. His work also continually deals with the isolation and self-destruction of people striving for an unreachable perfection, since this same perfection would mean stagnancy and therefore death. Anti-Catholic rhetoric is not uncommon.

"Es ist alles lächerlich, wenn man an den Tod denkt" (Everything is ridiculous, when one thinks of Death) was his comment when he received a minor Austrian national award in 1968, which resulted in one of the many public scandals he caused over the years and which became part of his fame. His novel *Holzfällen* (1984), for instance, could not be published for years due to a defamation claim by a former friend. Many of his plays—above all *Heldenplatz* (1988)—were met with criticism from many Austrians, who claimed they sullied Austria's reputation. One of the more controversial lines called Austria "a brutal and stupid nation a mindless, cultureless sewer which spreads its penetrating stench all over Europe." *Heldenplatz*, as well as the other plays Bernhard wrote in these years, were staged at Vienna's famous Burgtheater by the controversial director Claus Peymann.

Even in death Bernhard caused disturbance by his, as he supposedly called it, *posthumous literary emigration*, by disallowing all publication and stagings of his work within Austria's borders. The International Thomas Bernhard Foundation, established by his executor and half-brother Dr. Peter Fabjan, has subsequently made exceptions, although the German firm of Suhrkamp remains his principal publisher.

The correspondence between Bernhard and his publisher Siegfried Unseld from 1961 to 1989 about 500 letters has been published in December 2009 at Suhrkamp Verlag, Germany.[2]

Works (in translation)

Novels

- o *Gargoyles* (1970): Originally published as *Verstörung* (1967), translated by Richard Winston and Clara Winston.
- o *The Lime Works* (1973): Originally published as *Das Kalkwerk* (1970), translated by Sophie Wilkins.
- o *Correction* (1979): Originally published as *Korrektur* (1975), translated by Sophie Wilkins.
- o *Concrete* (1984): Originally published as *Beton* (1982), translated by David McLintock.
- o *Cutting Timber: An Irritation* (1985, novel): Originally published as *Holzfällen: Eine Erregung* (1984), translated by Ewald Osers. Also translated as *Woodcutters*, by David McLintock, in 1988.
- o *Wittgenstein's Nephew* (1988): Originally published as *Wittgensteins Neffe* (1982), translated by David McLintock.
- o *Old Masters: A Comedy* (1989): Originally published as *Alte Meister. Komödie* (1985), translated by Ewald Osers.

- *The Cheap-Eaters* (1990): Originally published as *Der Billigesser* (1980), translated by Ewald Osers.
- *The Loser* (1991): Originally published as *Der Untergeher* (1983), translated by Jack Dawson.
- *On The Mountain* (1991): Originally published as *In Der Höhe* (written 1959, published 1989), translated by Russell Stockman.
- *Yes* (1991): Originally published as *Ja* (1978), translated by Ewald Osers.
- *Extinction* (1995): Originally published as *Auslöschung* (1986), translated by David McLintock.
- *Three Novellas* (2003): Collects *Amras* (1964), *Playing Watten* (*Watten*, 1964) and *Walking* (*Gehen*, 1971). Translated by Peter Jansen and Kenneth J. Northcott.
- *Frost* (2006): Originally published in 1963, translated by Michael Hofmann.

Plays

- *The President and Eve of Retirement* (1982): Originally published as *Der Präsident* (1975) and *Vor dem Ruhestand. Eine Komödie von deutscher Seele* (1979), translated by Gitta Honegger.
- *Histrionics: Three Plays* (1990): Collects *A Party for Boris* (*Ein Fest für Boris*, 1968), *Ritter, Dene, Voss* (1984) and *Histrionics* (*Der Theatermacher*, 1984), translated by Peter Jansen and Kenneth Northcott.
- *Heldenplatz* (1988)
- *Over All the Mountain Tops* (2004): Originally published as *Über allen Gipfeln ist Ruh* (1981), translated by Michael Mitchell.

Miscellaneous

- *Gathering Evidence* (1985, memoir): Collects *Die Ursache* (1975), *Der Keller* (1976), *Der Atem* (1978), *Die Kälte* (1981) and *Ein Kind* (1982), translated by David McLintock.
- *The Voice Imitator* (1997, stories): Originally published as *Der Stimmenimitator* (1978), translated by Kenneth J. Northcott.[1]
- *In Hora Mortis / Under the Iron of the Moon* (2006, poetry): Collects *In Hora Mortis* (1958) and *Unter dem Eisen des Mondes* (1958), translated by James Reidel.

Further reading

- Gitta Honegger, *Thomas Bernhard: The Making of an Austrian*, Yale University Press, 2002, ISBN 0-300-08999-6
- JJ Long, *The Novels of Thomas Bernhard: Form and its Function*, Camden House Inc.,U.S., 2001, ISBN 1-57113-224-4
- Ruth Franklin, "The Art of Extinction," *The New Yorker,* December 25, 2006 and Jan 1, 2007

Reviews

- Updike, John (4 February 1985). "Books: Ungreat Lives". *The New Yorker* **60** (51): 94101. Review of *Concrete.*

See also (online edition)

- List of Austrian writers
- List of Austrians

References (URLs online)

- Website dedicated to Thomas Bernhard: works, essays, reviews
- List of works from the German wikipedia entry
- Thomas Bernhard's Heldenplatz in the press (German)
- Links to various related resources
- Random Evidence on Thomas Bernhard

- 1. *Thomas Bernhard: The Making of an Austrian*, Gitta Honegger, pp 61-63
- 2. *Der Briefwechsel Thomas Bernhard/Siegfried Unseld*, Suhrkamp Verlag, 2009-12-07

Websites (URLs online)

- Five stories from *The Voice Imitator.*
- Shooting of "Monologe auf Mallorca" Pictures by Stephan Mussil
- thomasbernhard.org - Thomas Bernhard in English: works, essays, reviews
- Salon.com review by Ben Marcus of *The Voice Imitator*
- *Bernhardiana*, a critical anthology on/of Thomas Bernhard (English/Italian)
- www.thomasbernhard.com Thomas Bernhard in Spanish.
- Thomas Bernhard for life A 1986 interview with Thomas Bernhard.

See also: Zuckerstätter

A hyperlinked version of this chapter is at http://booksllc.net?q=Thomas%5FBernhard

31

WALTER VON MOLO

Walter Ritter/Reichsritter von Molo (June 14, 1880, ternberk, Moravia October 27, 1958, Hechendorf, now Murnau am Staffelsee) was a Czech-born Austrian writer.

Life

Walter von Molo was born on 14 June 1880 in ternberk, Moravia. His youth was spent in Vienna, the capital of the Austro-Hungarian Empire. At high school he studied mechanical and electrical engineering; he married his first wife, Rosa Richter, in 1906, had a son and daughter, and worked until 1913 as an engineer in the Viennese Patent Office. Shortly before the outbreak of the First World War he moved to Berlin to be with his Bavarian parents and rediscover his German roots, just as Berlin was transforming itself into a cultural capital. It was there that he embarked upon his career as a writer.

His first works, published during and shortly after the war, were bestsellers, and he quickly became one of the most popular of all German-speaking authors of the first half of the century. The books included biographies of Friedrich Schiller, Frederick the Great, and Prince Eugen, as well as novels such as *Ein Volk wacht auf* ("A People Awakes", 1918-21). All were strongly marked by German nationalism.

In 1925 he divorced Rosa, and five years later married Annemarie Mummenhoff.

Molo was a founding member of the German PEN Club, and also, in 1926, of the Prussian Academy of Arts. From 1928 to 1930 he was chairman of the poetry section.

Molo remained a member of the academy after its purging of Jewish members, and on 15 March 1933 he signed a declaration pledging loyalty to the Nazi leaders. In October he was one of the 88 German writers who went so far as to subscribe to the Vow of Most Faithful Allegiance (*Gelöbnis treuester Gefolgschaft*) to Adolf Hitler. This was the same year that his two children left Germany. (Conrad returned in 1940; Trude did not.) In 1936 Molo wrote the screenplay for the film *Fridericus*, based on his novel of 1918. During the Second World War he wrote articles for the Nazi-controlled newspaper *Krakauer Zeitung* published in occupied Cracow.

Although Molo's biography of Frederick II of Prussia was praised by the Nazis, he nevertheless came under attack as *unvölkisch, ein Judenfreund* and *Pazifist* (he had, for example, effusively praised the work of E. M. Remarque), and there were attempts to push him from public life, with the banning of plays, and the suppression of certain books and their removal from libraries. In 1934, to avoid the public spotlight, he resigned from all the learned societies (except the Goethe Society) and moved to Murnau am Staffelsee, where he had bought property two years before. The idea of exile from Germany itself was unthinkable to him. House searches and defamatory articles continued, and in August 1939 he was denaturalised. As a result of the harassment, he destroyed, with the help of his second wife Anne Marie, a large part of his private library, including correspondence with Stefan Zweig, books by Thomas and Heinrich Mann bearing personal dedications, and many papers of his colleagues. All this potentially incriminating material ended up at the bottom of his garden pond. He was never placed under "protective custody" (*Schutzhaft*) as others were.

After the war he would become a bitter critic of the authors who had fled Germany. On 4 August 1945 an open letter from Molo to Thomas Mann, begging him to return from the US, was published in the *Hessischen Post* and other newspapers both in Germany and abroad: "Your people, hungering and suffering for a third of a century, has in its innermost core nothing in common with all the misdeeds and crimes, the shameful horrors and lies...." His sentiments were echoed by Frank Thiess, whose own piece would popularise the use of the phrase *innere Emigration* to describe the choice of some intellectuals to remain in Germany, a phrase Mann himself had used in 1933. Mann responded, on 28 September, in a statement which caused general indignation in Germany, that new books "published in Germany between 1933 and 1945, can be called less than worthless", that exile had been a sacrifice and not an evasion, and that the nation as a whole did bear responsibility for atrocities committed by its leaders.[1]

This unleashed a huge controversy between the exiled authors and the ones who had chosen to remain. Molo claimed that writers who had abandoned Germany forfeited the right to shape its future.

Despite his appointment as honorary chairman of the German Society of Authors, he did not regain his former prominence. He died on 27 October 1958, and his remains were interred in what is now Molo Park in Murnau. Rosa died in 1970, and Annemarie in 1983.

Works

Stories and novels

- *Klaus Tiedmann der Kaufmann*, 1909
- *Ums Menschentum. Ein Schillerroman*, 1912
- *Im Titanenkampf. Ein Schillerroman*, 1913
- *Der Hochzeitsjunker. Ein Rennroman*, 1913
- *Die Freiheit. Ein Schillerroman*, 1914
- *Den Sternen zu. Ein Schillerroman*, 1916
- *Der Große Fritz im Krieg*, 1917
- *Schiller in Leipzig*, 1917
- *Die ewige Tragikomödie. Novellistische Studien 1906-1912*, 1917
- *Fridericus*, novel, 1918
- *Luise*, novel, 1919
- *Auf der rollenden Erde*, novel, 1923
- *Vom alten Fritz. 4 Erzählungen aus dem Leben des großen Königs*, 1924
- *Bodenmatz*, novel, 1925
- *Im ewigen Licht*, novel, 1926
- *Die Legende vom Herrn*, 1927
- *Hans Amrung und seine Frau und andere Novellen*, 1927
- *Mensch Luther*, novel, 1928
- *Die Scheidung. Ein Roman unserer Zeit*, 1929
- *Ein Deutscher ohne Deutschland. Ein Friedrich List-Roman*, 1931
- *Holunder in Polen*, novel, 1933
- *Der kleine Held*, novel, 1934
- *Eugenio von Savoy. Heimlicher Kaiser des Reichs*, novel, 1936
- *Geschichte einer Seele*, 1938
- *Das kluge Mädchen*, novel, 1940
- *Der Feldmarschall*, 1940
- *Sie sollen nur des Gesetzes spotten*, stories, 1943
- *Im Sommer. Eine Lebenssonate, 2 Erzählungen*, 1943
- *Der Menschenfreund*, novel, 1948
- *Die Affen Gottes. Roman der Zeit*, 1950

Plays

- *Das gelebte Leben*, drama in 4 acts, 1911
- *Die Mutter*, drama in 4 acts, 1914
- *Der Infant der Menschheit*, drama in 3 acts, 1916
- *Die Erlösung der Ethel*, tragedy in 4 acts, 1917
- *Friedrich Staps. Ein deutsches Volksstück in 4 Aufzügen*, 1918
- *Der Hauch im All*, tragedy in 3 acts, 1918
- *Die helle Nacht*, play in 3 acts, 1920
- *Till Lausebums*, romantic comedy in 3 acts, 1921
- *Lebensballade*, a play in 12 scenes, 1924
- *Ordnung im Chaos*, play in 8 tableaux, 1928
- *Friedrich List. Ein deutsches Prophetenleben in 3 Aufzügen*, 1934

Screenplays

- *Fridericus* (D, 1936), directed by Johannes Meyer, with Otto Gebühr, Hilde Körber, Lil Dagover, Agnes Straub, Käthe Haack and others
- *Der unendliche Weg* (D, 1942/43), directed by Hans Schweikart, with Eugen Klöpfer, Eva Immermann, Hedwig Wangel, Alice Treff and others

Other writings

- *Deutsches Volk. Ein Flugblatt in jedes Haus*, 1914
- *Als ich die bunte Mütze trug. Deutsch-österreichische Studenten-Erinnerungen*, 1914
- *An unsere Seelen. Drei Flugblätter auf das Kriegsjahr 1914-1915*, 1915
- *Deutschland und Oesterreich. Kriegsaufsätze*, 1915
- *Deutsch sein heißt Mensch sein! Notschrei aus deutscher Seele*, 1915
- *An Frederik van Eeden und Romain Rolland. Offener Brief*, 1915
- *Sprüche der Seele*, 1916
- *Im Schritt der Jahrhunderte. Geschichtliche Bilder*, 1917
- *Italien. Erlebnisse Deutscher in Italien*, 1921
- *Im Zwielicht der Zeit. Bilder aus unseren Tagen*, 1922
- *Der deutschen Jugend gesagt*, 1929
- *Zwischen Tag und Traum. Gesammelte Reden und Aufsätze*, 1930
- *Deutsche Volksgemeinschaft. Ansprache am 22. März 1932 in Weimar*, 1932
- *Wie ich Deutschland möchte. Eine Rede über Friedrich List*, 1932
- *Lob des Leides*, 1947
- *Zu neuem Tag. Ein Lebensbericht*, 1950
- *So wunderbar ist das Leben. Erinnerungen und Begegnungen*, 1957
- *Wo ich Frieden fand. Erlebnisse und Erinnerungen*, 1959

See also (online edition)

- Gottfried Benn
- Thomas Mann
- Frank Thiess

Notes

- 1. Stephen Brockmann. *German literary culture at the zero hour.* Camden House, Rochester, 2004.

References (URLs online)

- Werner von Berge: *Der lange Weg aus dem Exil. Die Diskussion um die Heimkehr aus dem Exil am Beispiel Thomas Manns und des Streites zwischen "innerer" und "äußerer" Emigration. 1945-1949.* Magisterarbeit, Universität Frankfurt am Main 1984
- Babette Dietrich: *"Ein Auftrag von höherer Macht ...".* *Walter von Molo und die Mainzer Literaturklasse 1949-1956.* (= Edition Wissenschaft; Reihe Germanistik; 7). Tectum-Verlag, Marburg 1995, ISBN 3-89608-877-7
- Hanns Martin Elster: *Walter von Molo und sein Schaffen.* Langen, München 1920
- Franz Camillo Munck: *Walter von Molo. Der Dichter und das Leben.* (= Vom Herzschlag meines Volkes; 2). Koch, Leipzig 1924
- Gustav Christian Rassy: *Walter von Molo. Ein Dichter des deutschen Menschen.* Bohn, Leipzig 1936
- Karl O. Vitense: *Walter von Molo. Das Wesen des Schriftstellers.* Dissertation, Universität Leipzig 1936

Websites (URLs online)

- Walter von Molo in the German National Library catalogue (German)
- Eintrag zu Walter von Molo im *Projekt Historischer Roman* (Datenbank der Universität Innsbruck)
- Eintrag zu Walter von Molo bei filmportal.de
- Walter von Molo at the Internet Movie Database
- Molo Park

A hyperlinked version of this chapter is at http://booksllc.net?q=Walter%5Fvon%5FMolo

---

32

WARIS DIRIE

Waris Dirie (Somali: *Waris Diiriye*, Arabic:) (born in 1965) is a Somali model, author, actress and human rights activist.

Early years

Waris Dirie was born into a nomadic clan in Gaalkacyo, Somalia in 1965.[1] At the age of thirteen, she fled her family in order to escape an arranged marriage to a much older man. She landed in London, England, where she lived with and worked for wealthy relatives. Waris later worked at a local McDonald's, trying to make ends meet after a falling out with her hosts.[2]

Career

By chance, Waris was discovered by photographer Terence Donovan, who helped secure for her the cover of the 1987 Pirelli calendar. From there, her modeling career took off, scoring advertisements for top designers such as Chanel, Levi's, L'Oréal and Revlon.

In 1987, Waris played a minor role in the James Bond movie *The Living Daylights*. She also appeared on the runways of London, Milan, Paris and New York City, and in fashion magazines such as *Elle*, *Glamour* and *Vogue*. This was followed in 1995 by a BBC documentary entitled *A Nomad in New York* about her modeling career.

In 1997, at the height of her modeling career, Waris spoke for the first time with Laura Ziv of the women's magazine *Marie Claire* about the female genital mutilation (FGM) that she had undergone as a child, an interview which received worldwide media coverage. That same year, Waris became a UN ambassador for the abolition of FGM, and later paid her mother a visit in her native Somalia.

In 1998, Waris authored her first book, *Desert Flower*, an autobiography which went on to become an international bestseller.[2] She later released other successful books including *Desert Dawn*, *Letter To My Mother*, and *Desert Children*, the latter of which was launched in tandem with a European campaign against FGM.

In 2009, a feature-length film loosely-based on Waris' book *Desert Flower* was released, with the Ethiopian supermodel Liya Kebede playing her.[3]

Attack and disappearance

In March 2004, Waris was attacked in her home in Vienna, Austria. Paulo Augusto, a 26-year-old Portuguese man, was held in custody after having apparently stalked her some 1,000 miles across Europe, eventually gaining access to her apartment by climbing through a neighbour's window. *"She was so frightened and in shock that she let him in,"* a police spokesman said. Dirie apparently suffered minor injuries when her assailant threw her to the floor. The attacker then left in a taxi, only to return later on foot to smash one of the building's ground-floor windows. He was arrested when neighbours called the police,[4] and was later given a five month suspended sentence by an Austrian court.[5] It was reported that the suspect had met Dirie six months earlier when his brother was working at her previous residence in Wales. He later broke into that home and stole items of her clothing.[6]

In another incident, during the early hours of Wednesday, March 5, 2008, Waris went missing for three days while staying in Brussels, Belgium. She was found alive on Friday, March 7, 2008 by a Brussels policeman. A few days later, she told Austrian media that she had been kidnapped and held by a taxi-driver who also tried to rape her.[5]

Personal life

Contrary to popular belief, Waris is not related to fellow Somali model Iman. In her book *Desert Flower*, Waris states that Iman's mother was good friends with her aunt, a relative with whom Waris once lived during her time in London.

In March 2005, Waris acquired Austrian citizenship.[7]

Humanitarian work, awards and honours

In 1997, Waris abandoned her modeling career to focus on her work against female circumcision. That same year, she was appointed UN Special Ambassador for the Elimination of Female Genital Mutilation.[8][9] In 2002, she founded the Waris Dirie Foundation in Vienna, Austria, an organization aimed at raising awareness regarding the dangers surrounding FGM. Waris followed that in January 2009 with the establishment of the PPR Foundation for Womens Dignity and Rights, an organization she founded along with French tycoon François-Henri Pinault (CEO of PPR) and his wife, Hollywood actress Salma Hayek.[10] Waris has also started the Desert Dawn Foundation, which raises money for schools and clinics in her native Somalia.[2]

Waris has received many prizes and awards for her humanitarian work and books including:

- o "Woman of the Year Award" by Glamour Magazine (2000)[11]
- o "Corine Award" of the umbrella association of the German bookselling trade (2002)[12]
- o "Womens World Award" from former Russian President, Mikhail Gorbachev (2004)[13]
- o "Bishop Óscar Romero Award" by the Catholic Church (2005)
- o "Chevalier de la Légion dHonneur" (2007) from the French President, Nicolas Sarkozy[14]
- o Prix des Générations by the World Demographic Association (2007) [15]
- o Martin Buber Gold Medal from the Euriade Foundation (2008) [16] founded by Werner Janssen in 1981.

Books and filmography

Books

- o *Desert Flower*
- o *Desert Dawn*
- o *Desert Children*
- o *Desert Children*
- o *Letter To My Mother*
- o *Letter To My Mother*

Films

- o *The Living Daylights* (1987)

Notes

- 1. Babor - Waris Dirie profile
- 2. Somalia's Desert Flower Time Magazine July 7th, 2002
- 3. Model Liya Kebede to star in 'Flower'
- 4. Somalian-born author attacked by stalker The Guardian March 11th, 2004
- 5. Former Model Waris Dirie Found Alive in Brussels Fox News March 7th, 2008
- 6. Model's stalker had previous arrests BBC News March 11th, 2004
- 7. Former Supermodel Waris Dirie Gets Austrian Citizenship
- 8. Messengers of Peace and Goodwill Ambassadors at the United Nations
- 9. UNFPA Goodwill ambassador, Waris Dirie, wins award UNFPA - United Nations Population Fund April 17th, 2001
- 10. PPR Foundation for Women's Rights and Dignity
- 11. UNECA
- 12. Corine Award Corine Award 2002 Waris Dirie for *Desert Dawn*
- 13. Women's World Awards
- 14. Communiqué de la Présidence de la République annonçant la remise de décoration par M. Nicolas SARKOZY, Président de la République July 12th, 2007
- 15. World Demographic Association
- 16. Martin Buber Foundation Martin Buber Gold Medal 2007 for Waris Dirie

Websites (URLs online)

- Waris Dirie Foundation
- Waris Dirie at Fashion Model Directory
- PPR-Foundation
- Reader's Digest version of Desert Flower

A hyperlinked version of this chapter is at http://booksllc.net?q=Waris%5FDirie

INDEX

CPSIA information can be obtained at www.ICGtesting.com
Printed in the USA
BVOW041602241212

309042BV00002B/126/P